embarrassment

"Why has no one written about this subject before? Every teacher should read this book."
—**Michael G. Thompson,** coauthor of *Raising Cain*

(embarrassment)

AND THE EMOTIONAL **UNDERLIFE OF LEARNING**

THOMAS NEWKIRK

HEINEMANN
PORTSMOUTH, NH

Heinemann
361 Hanover Street
Portsmouth, NH 03801–3912
www.heinemann.com

Offices and agents throughout the world

The author and publisher wish to thank those who have generously given permission to reprint borrowed material:

Figure 2–1: Excerpt from "Academia, Love Me Back" by Tiffany Martinez from the blog *Tiffany Martínez: A Journal*, posted October 27, 2016. Reprinted with permission from the author.

Credits continue on page vi.

Cataloging-in-Publication Data is on file at the Library of Congress.
ISBN: 978-0-325-08877-8

Editor: Margaret LaRaia
Production: Victoria Merecki
Cover and interior designs: Suzanne Heiser
Typesetter: Valerie Levy, Drawing Board Studios LLC
Manufacturing: Steve Bernier

Printed in the United States of America on acid-free paper
21 20 19 18 RWP 2 3 4 5

CONTENTS

Credits, continued from page iv:

Excerpt from "Organizing Classroom Instruction That Supports ELLs: Promoting Student Engagement and Oral Language Development" by Julie Nora and Julie E. Wollman (2007) in *One Classroom, Many Learners: Best Literacy Practices for Today's Multilingual Classrooms* edited by Julie Coppola and Elizabeth V. Primas. Copyright © 2009 by the International Literacy Association, Inc. Published by the International Literacy Association. Reprinted with permission from the Editor.

The Blank Turn: Originally appeared in the online commentary "Teachers: Know When to Stop Talking" by Thomas Newkirk in *Education Week*, July 28, 2015. Copyright © 2015 by Thomas Newkirk.

Figure 6–1: From *Which One Doesn't Belong?* by Christopher Danielson. Copyright © 2016 by Christopher Danielson. Reproduced with permission of Stenhouse Publishers. www.stenhouse.com

Toward Self-Generosity: From "Speaking Up . . . & Talking Back" by Thomas Newkirk in the Summer 2015 (online only) edition of *Educational Leadership*, 72(9). Copyright © 2015 by ASCD. Reprinted with permission.

Image credit:
page 117: © Everett Historical/Shutterstock

ACKNOWLEDGMENTS

A major theme of this book is the importance of seeking help—and I was a beneficiary of great generosity. My editor Margaret LaRaia at Heinemann was a consistent supporter, and at times she had more faith in this project than I did. Not only did she encourage me, but she truly understood what I was attempting, and pointed me toward resources that could help me.

David Pillemer met me regularly for coffee and tutorials on episodic memory. I feel like I owe him tuition money. He made my border crossings into memory studies possible—and I am so grateful to have been introduced to his own generative work.

I had really excellent readers along the way. Tomasen Carey read a very early version of the book and gave me confidence that it might work. Later I benefitted from very thoughtful readings from Peter Johnston, Steve Mahoney, and Lad Tobin. Lad also read an earlier prospectus and gave great feedback. He has been an invaluable reader and supportive friend over the years. I also received encouraging feedback from Katherine Bomer, Kim Cahill, and Brett Whitmarsh.

In the book I made extensive use of interviews with Ian Fleischer, Tracy Zager, Mike Anderson, Julie Nora, Andrea Rousso, Tim Churchard, Molly Tetreault, Kenny Rotner, Denise Reddington, Melanie Sims, Sam Fuld, Christina Ortmeier-Hooper, Rich Kent, Jennie Marshall, Lea Maurer, and David Pillemer. Thanks to you all.

I want to express my deepest appreciation to Edie Davis Quinn for help with permissions; to Suzanne Heiser for her wonderful work on the cover and interior design; to Kim Cahill for her commitment to the promotion of *Embarrassment*; to Cindy Ann Black for her copyediting (sorry I gave you so much work!); to Brett Whitmarsh for his help with social media; and to Victoria Merecki who oversaw production. A special and continuing thanks to Vicki Boyd, the General Manager of Heinemann, who is such an insightful supporter of Heinemann authors. We are so lucky to have her at the helm.

To my wife, Beth, thanks for listening to so much of this, and every now and then asking, "So what does that have to do with embarrassment?"

I

UNDERLIFE

CHAPTER 1

The Emotional Underlife of Learning

> *Out of the crooked timber of humanity, no straight thing was ever made.*
>
> —**IMMANUEL KANT,** *IDEA FOR A UNIVERSAL HISTORY WITH A COSMOPOLITAN AIM*

I'll go first.

A memory from first grade—sixty-two years ago. We had what was called "rhythm band"—as I recall some of us (actually most of us) had sticks, some hand bells, some metal triangles, and tambourines. The teacher would set a rhythm and various groups would come in singly and together. The theory, which never made sense to me, was that making these sounds, to a beat or rhythm, would awaken our love of music.

At one point she asked if any of us wanted to direct the band, and unaccountably I raised my hand. Probably I misheard the question—thinking she was asking if anyone wanted to go to the bathroom. I was that drifty kind of kid. I knew I had made a mistake, because I had no clue how all this worked, but to back down would be humiliating. I recall my slow walk up to the front of my classmates, and the teacher handing me the baton.

I took a breath and pointed at the sticks, and we started—clack, clack, clack, clack. I didn't know what else to do. I just kept pointing at the damn sticks, more clacking. All my classmates, the combined first grades, virtually everyone I knew, were watching me, wondering if there would be more to this. I didn't know how or why to do anything more, how to change rhythm or shift instruments—and felt frozen. When would this end? Finally the teacher stopped it all, thanked me and I slunk back to my place in the band.

I can still feel the panic of that minute or so—though I'm sure everyone else forgot about it quickly. It is what psychologists call a "flashbulb memory"—they are so "present" in our memories that we often shift into the present tense when we retell them ("So I walk to the front of the class. . . ."). Paradoxically, as I think about it now, the teacher may have been impressed that I at least tried. But the feeling of panic is still there, and I revisit that moment occasionally in wakeful moments at night.

It is that kind of feeling that this book is about.

I want to start with this feeling in the gut, to explore the subterranean domain of emotion, failure, and embarrassment—working my way up to teaching practices (I promise). I want to do this for several reasons. One is my own estrangement from much of the upbeat, motivational descriptions of teaching practices, where everything seems to run with machinelike efficiency. I don't see reflected back to me the anxieties, hesitancies, frustrations, and yes failures that take up so much of my own mental space. The emotional underlife of teaching and learning are simply airbrushed out of the picture. Everything is depressingly and uniformly successful.

It's not that I don't learn from these accounts or that I don't admire those who create them. And it could be that those who write them don't feel what I feel, so they are not intentionally leaving out these subterranean feelings. If you are one of these people, I suggest you stop reading now and see if you can get a refund on this book.

This emotional underside has not been given due attention, and as a result it is possible, indeed inevitable, that these darker emotions can be taken as evidence of personal inadequacy, and therefore hidden. Years ago, I wrote an essay, "Silences in Our Teaching Stories: What We Leave Out and Why" (1992). It was my small effort to open the door to a type of more candid talk about the emotional struggles of teaching. I began by quoting a great piece of writing by one of our writing institute participants, Karen Wienhold. She wrote about how she failed to feel affection for her first child in the month after her birth—and how damning that was for her as a mother to feel this, how literally unspeakable. In fact, that piece of writing was her first admission. Thankfully she established an emotional connection as the baby grew more responsive, but that first month was an emotional desert. She violated an emotional orthodoxy, that mothers are overjoyed by their new infants, instantly rapturous. And she didn't fit. Her coming forward was a model for what I wanted to do.

I am convinced this silence is damaging. About the same time I was writing that essay, I remember going to a session, arranged by a couple of PhD students, who brought together psychologists and writing teachers to talk about what we had in common. At one point someone asked one of the therapists: "What do you do if you are bored by what your client is saying?"

There was a hush in the room, and I was expecting the therapist to say something like "I don't get bored" or "If you get bored, you are not paying attention." But he didn't say either of these things. He said something like: "Of course, you get bored. And when that happens you have to ask yourself why you are bored. It may be the client is simply repeating herself from session to session—and that may be something you have to address." This was an illuminating moment for me—he went on that it would be a mistake to pretend this boredom didn't exist, or shouldn't exist, or that he was a bad therapist because he felt it. The true mistake would be to fail to deal with it.

I have had interesting reactions when I tell people I am writing a book on embarrassment and learning. First, there is a puzzled look, like isn't literacy your thing. Then, within seconds, there is a story—a caustic remark from a teacher that still stings decades later, the shame of oral reading, the terror of public speaking. Alive and vivid in memory.

It seems to me that embarrassment (or fear thereof) is one of those big facts of learning—or not learning—and that it deserves attention. It interferes, inhibits, forces misjudgments. I have seen it shut down Vygotsky's famous zone of proximal development into nothing—any risk, any uncertainty closes down student effort. And embarrassment doesn't even need an audience: no one needs to watch us struggle with an eighth-grade algebra problem. We perform for ourselves, often the harshest of audiences.

The Crooked Timber

Education, it seems, often proceeds on the assumption of rational self-advancement. You want to be "college and career ready"? Here is what you need to do. Like traditional economics, it is based on the premise that if the incentives are right, we will act in our self-interest. But the field of behavioral economics, made available to the general reader in Daniel Kahneman's *Thinking, Fast and Slow* (2011), shows the consistent irrational biases that cause people to make imprudent financial decisions. For example, in my early career I refused to put any of my retirement money in stocks—even though the recommendation was to put at least 50 percent in them. Why? Because my most salient and vivid image of stock investing was the Crash of 1929—all of those men who lost everything jumping out of windows. This cost me plenty.

One rational image of learning is Carol Dweck's (2008) hugely influential distinction between the "fixed mindset" and the "growth mindset." Her formulation is so widely known that there is probably no need to summarize. But in a nutshell, she argues (and provides evidence) that we can be limited if we see ourselves as having fixed, stable traits like intelligence or imagination or creativity. We are far better off if we could see ourselves as more fluid, in process—to see intelligence not as something you have but as a capacity to engage in problem-solving, to adopt what John Dewey called an "attitude of suspended conclusion" (1910, 13).

Her approach, particularly as it has entered schools, is highly rational, self-evidently the way we *should* want to go. My ideal approach to a difficult algebra problem should logically be to slow down, lay it out, work a proof, test it a second time. To be calm the whole way. To do all this without a sense of anxiety or embarrassment because I was not putting any fixed identity at risk. I'll admit that this is the ideal state of learning, emptying out the emotional baggage that interferes. This is how we would want to be, if we could.

But what gets in the way? It seems to me it is more than the choice of the wrong mindset, or the ways in which teachers give praise. It is something bigger than that. Dweck, in a revisiting of her work, distances herself from the popularizations of her work, stressing that achieving a growth mindset is "a journey not a proclamation" (2015). She also acknowledges that we all are susceptible to fixed mindset reactions to difficult problems and that a key trait in developing a growth mindset is recognizing these fixed mindset triggers—panic, defensiveness, anxiety. We can say that failure is healthy—just as we can say that pain is often necessary for health—but we instinctively want to avoid both. Just how we can achieve this more resilient and effective approach to difficulty and failure—the help we need, the voices we need to hear, the barriers we need to overcome—will be the subject of this book.

I'll point to three self-evident facts of social life that get in the way of our rationality—the first is that we "perform" a self in social encounters.

In his classic and best-known book, *The Presentation of Self in Everyday Life* (1959), Erving Goffman makes a compelling case that we are *performers* in all social encounters, and all performances entail risks. We perform as parents, students, passengers on the bus. He quotes sociologist Robert Park on the centrality of enacting a role and how these roles define the self we want to be:

> It is probably no mere historical accident that the word person, in its first meaning, is a mask. It is rather recognition of the fact that everyone is always and everywhere, more or less consciously, playing a role. . . . It is in these roles that we know each other; it is in these roles that we know ourselves.
>
> In a sense, and in so far as the mask represents the conception we have formed of ourselves—the role we are striving to live up to—this mask is the truer self, the self we would like to be. In the end, our conception of our role becomes second nature and an integral part of our personality. We come into the world as individuals, achieve character, and become persons. (Goffman 1959, 19–20)

Goffman (and Park) locate selfhood, not in a presocial identity, but in the acquisition of performative competence, the capacity to effortlessly take on multiple roles. When we are in situations when this social competence fails us, we lose a sense of who we are.

> "Everyone is always and everywhere, more or less consciously, playing a role. . . . It is in these roles that we know each other; it is in these roles that we know ourselves."

But there is something perilous in this conception. As performers there is the constant possibility of misperforming, providing what Goffman calls "discrepant information." For example, if a waitress rolls her eyes as she waits for a diner to make a food choice, she is undermining her role; she is not presenting herself as totally focused on fulfilling that person's wishes. Embarrassment typically involves this discrepant information.

Take this banal example, which occurred at a reception after the wedding of my nephew. I hadn't attended the dinner the night before the wedding, so the bride's family was something of a mystery to me. I was speaking to the bride's mother and I commented on a wonderful toast given by a man I took to be her husband. "My husband?" she asked with a wry smile. "That was my brother." It turned out her husband, ex-husband actually, was long out of the picture, virtually a nonperson in this family, like one of those Soviet commissars who disappear from podium photographs. My not knowing that was "discrepant information."

When mistakes like this occur, there is social pain not only for the culprit but also for the audience. Just as there is the danger of secondary cigarette smoke, there is secondary embarrassment. As humans we operate on cooperative principles; we assume and desire mutual competence in role taking. Take as another example an interview situation, and imagine it is going badly. The candidate is nervous, flustered, and can manage only brief answers to the questions posed. This is excruciating for the candidate, but uncomfortable for the interviewer as well. So what happens? The interviewer may decide to take longer narrative terms describing the company, placing the candidate in the role of listener. Goffman would call this redefining the "situation definition" so that both participants can effectively play their roles.

It might be objected that in most social encounters we don't *feel* that we are performing. Take something as simple as walking down a street in Boston. We are not conscious of the rules we are "naturally" following. These rules might include passing on the right when someone approaches, not entering in to conversation when you are walking abreast of someone (the rule is different in my less crowded small town), keeping with the flow of pedestrian traffic, not stopping abruptly, feeling free to disobey the walk light if there is no oncoming traffic, not touching or bumping other pedestrians. If, for example, you should trip and fall—as my wife did once on crowded Washington Street—you become acutely aware of misperforming before an audience, and most likely feel the embarrassment flooding in before the pain of the fall—and remember it longer.

It might also be argued that it is possible to retreat from the "stages" where we perform, to nonpublic areas, what Goffman calls the "backstage"—places that are "safe." For example, in the traditional high school teachers' room, it's OK to talk directly about frustrations and individual students in a way that would be inappropriate, even offensive, outside it. But the teachers' room is also a stage with its own rules, taboos, and hierarchies. In the teachers' room of my first school, the topic of the day would *always* be the performance of the Big Bad Bruins of the early

'70s—we assiduously avoided discussing real teaching. What we have is a virtual infinite regression of stages—and, at the end of the day, in the solitude of our study when we reflect on the day, we may still be performing to ourselves, assessing how we have done, measuring our actions against the ideals we set for ourselves. Even in the privacy of that moment we are not offstage.

> In all social encounters we play roles that we desire to perform competently. Embarrassment typically involves this discrediting information that undermines our performances.

So we might define the performative principle this way: *in all social encounters we play roles that we desire to perform competently. Embarrassment typically involves this discrediting information that undermines our performances.*

The second fact is this: we tend to have unrealistically positive self-evaluations. We all seem to live in Garrison Keillor's Lake Wobegone where we and all our children are above average. In one survey of Australian workers, 89 percent rated themselves above average (only 1 percent rated themselves as below average!). We are all better than average drivers, students, lovers, thinkers. We like the look we see in the mirror and claim that we just don't photograph well because photographs don't match the image we see. It has been conclusively demonstrated that we are biased toward the letters in our name (not making this up) (Leary 2004, 62). As the preacher says in Ecclesiastes: "Vanity of vanities, vanity of vanities! All is vanity."

It follows that if we have an inflated view of self, if we see ourselves as more competent, attractive, intelligent than by any objective measure we are—then we can misjudge how much we have to lose.

> People like to think of themselves as better than most other people, so when failure or disgrace arrives, their self-image sustains a serious blow. They keep their egos defended as long as possible through various self-serving tactics, but when the walls are finally breached, the ego's defenses temporarily collapse. (Leary 2004, 63)

So we might describe the vanity principle this way: *humans habitually tend to overestimate their capacities—which leads to dissonance and discomfort when we confront situations that fail to support this self-image.*

Humans habitually tend to overestimate their capacities—which leads to dissonance and discomfort when we confront situations that fail to support this self-image.

To some degree these illusions, this overestimation, can be an asset as Shelly Taylor argues in her book, *Positive Illusions: Creative Self-Deception and the Healthy Mind* (1989). Like Leary she sees this positive bias as part of normal human thought that helps us through difficult situations. One thinks of one of Ronald Reagan's favorite stories about the boy who was given a pile of manure for his birthday. He begins shoveling, and when asked why he is shoveling, he responds: "I know there is a pony under here somewhere."

Add in a third principle. Let's call it the awkwardness principle: *any act of learning requires us to suspend a natural tendency to want to appear fully competent. We need to accept the fact that we will be awkward, that our first attempts at a new skill will, at best, be only partial successes. Moreover we need to allow this awkwardness to be viewed by some mentor who can offer feedback as we open ourselves up for instruction.* There is a vulnerability here—it is the irreducible, unavoidable condition for learning. Viewed this way, the learning situation stands apart from the normal state of public performance, outside our "comfort zone," exposed.

These three principles can be a potent combination. As Goffman reminds us we are always on stage, in a role, and at risk (even slight) of misperforming. And, because we overestimate ourselves, habitually, we can overestimate the consequences of our discrepant performance, or more likely misjudge the performance entirely, holding ourselves to a standard that no one else expects, or making it more significant to others than it realistically is. And because we must misperform publicly before we are competent, the very act of learning can be fraught—or avoided.

To put it a different way, the growth mindset can promote a fluid sense of self, one in which the only fixed point is our sense of process, of our capacity to accept challenges and learn from them. But the countervailing force is our sense of *identity,* the image we create of ourselves, strengths and weaknesses. This is not as fluid, or barely fluid at all. It is shaped by our histories—past successes and failures, like my own unpleasant experience leading the rhythm band. It is shaped by past praise and criticism, voices in our head we can still hear. We want to protect this identity, at times even when it is not working well for us.

When this sense of self is severely challenged, the effect can be truly upsetting, demoralizing. There is a great deal of happy talk these days about welcoming failure, the need for failure, and learning from failure, even the gift of failure—but this tribute comes primarily from people who generally succeed. In his wonderful book, *Lives on the Boundary* (1989), Mike Rose offers vivid portraits of high-achieving high school students, demoralized by the demands of introductory courses at a large university like UCLA where Rose teaches. Imagine, he asks us, the student who worked hard through high school, received top grades, awards, and finally receives his reward, admission.

> You are finally sitting in the lecture hall you have been preparing to sit in for years. You have been the good student, perhaps even the star—you are to be the engineer, the lawyer, the doctor. Your parents have knocked themselves out for you. And you can't get what some man is saying in an *introductory* course. You're not what you thought you were. The alien voice of the lecturer is telling you that something central to your being is, after all, a wish spun in the night, a ruse, the mist and vapor of sleep. (1989, 174)

My own story is a version of this demoralization, when a paper I wrote for my freshman writing course at Oberlin was picked for class critique. We were assigned the task of illustrating an abstract concept with concrete examples—I picked courage and used as two of my examples, "Flea" Roberts, a tiny running back who played for the Cleveland Browns, and Robert E. Lee (courageous for his surrender). I can now only imagine the amusement of my professor as he saw those two examples in proximity.

It was a Friday afternoon, and I was expecting praise for all the verbal tricks and good vocabulary that had served me so well in high school. But it soon became apparent none of this would happen. Papers were presented anonymously, which effectively silenced me. The paper was shredded sentence by sentence, until the class ended—I clearly recollect at 3:30. At least I could escape to the weekend. But the professor concluded the class by saying there were still problems with the paper that needed to be discussed, so we would take up the critique session on Monday. I heard the same voice Rose described: "You're not what you thought you were."

My colleague David Pillemer has done extensive interviews about vivid, often humiliating and embarrassing, memories of schooling. He finds that we recall humiliation with greater vividness than any other kind of memory, even positive ones. In the same semester as my paper critique I received my first F on a history exam—and at the end of one question, which asked us to apply a Marxist interpretation to some event, the professor wrote on my bluebook, "This is more bull than knowledge." It surely was that, but not intentionally—Marxism was only a name for me, a vocab word. I still have a visual image of that comment. I can see still see his blue handwriting—and the handwriting on the wall. *You're not what you thought you were.*

> If we can take on a topic like embarrassment and shame, we can come to a richer, more honest, more enabling sense of who we are and what we can do.

I want to be clear—I do not for a moment concede that examining this emotional underside of learning leads to a diminished view of ourselves. Or to pessimism or defeatism. I contend the exact opposite—that if we can take on a topic like embarrassment and shame, we can come to a richer, more honest, more enabling sense of who we are and what we can do. It may be that "nothing straight" can come from the "crooked timber of mankind." But that crookedness, that irrationality, the emotional baggage we carry, that learning history is what defeats all the rational schemes that proliferate. It defeats that dream of the systems-builders for absolute prediction—if we do *x*, you will do *y*.

In his great story, "Notes from the Underground," Dostoevsky transformed the newly built iron and glass Crystal Palace in London into a symbol—of the rational control of human behavior. In the future, it seemed to promise, human existence could conform to universal rational principles (Marxism would become one of those systems). To which Dostoevsky countered that at the core we are not rational, reasonable, and will not submit to rational systems.

> You believe in a palace of crystal that can never be destroyed—a palace at which one will not be able to put out one's tongue or make a long nose on the sly. And perhaps that is just why I am afraid of this edifice, that it is of crystal and can never be destroyed and that one cannot put one's tongue out at it even on the sly. (1960, 151)

We have many versions of this Crystal Palace in education, a virtual alphabet soup (CBE, NCLB, RTI, CCSS, PACE, etc.) promising results so long as there is "fidelity" (an interesting term) in enactment. If we find the right procedure, the "best practice," if we do the *x*, we can promise the *y*. The emotional life of teacher and student can be overwritten.

I argue that we cannot wish away this irrationality, this predisposition to embarrassment, shame, avoidance—to a distorted sense of self. It is our human inheritance. We cannot cast a spell so that that incidents of humiliation don't come flooding back. The blows to our identity, like the ones Mike Rose describes, are truly painful and difficult to process, and impossible to forget. What we can do is be truthful, to tell our stories, be honest about our histories, or as honest as we can be. To not pretend. To reject unattainable models. We can also tell stories, unvarnished, about how we dealt with this pain and disappointment—recognizing all along that falling short is an inevitable part of living.

We cannot eradicate our own irrationality—but we can acknowledge it, and acknowledge that the emotional underlife of teaching and learning deserves as much attention as technique or procedure. When, for example, we look at the gruesome statistics of young teachers leaving the profession, how much of that exit is due to a sense of failure, of not living up to expectations, of private embarrassment, that finds no outlet in honest discussion?

The theme of this book is that we have two systems of response to psychological and physical threats—one that is embodied, unverbalized, emotional, instantaneous, and deeply rooted in our evolutionary history. The other is explicit, verbal, and rational. Daniel Kahneman (2011) has called these two types of response fast and slow thinking. We cannot escape this fast embodied response. We cannot unembarrass ourselves when we forget a name we should know, or fail to make the foul shot that would win the game. There is not time or opportunity for language to slip in and prevent the discomfort. It all happens too fast, the flush in the face, the hollowness behind our knees. I don't believe we can even *will* ourselves to forget these moments, as memory itself may be biased to retain these negative recollections.

The slower, delayed verbal analysis is the best resource we have to cope. It cannot eradicate the pain of social failure, but it can mitigate it and bring in perspective and a more realistic assessment of the consequences of our failures—which we invariably exaggerate. It can also be used proactively to help anticipate difficulty and model how to cope with it. Inchoate feeling and shame can translated into shared narratives, plans of action, and even humor. We can learn to talk to ourselves in more generous ways.

Enough silence. Enough.

(CHAPTER 2)

The Need for Embarrassment

> *Were they ashamed because of the abomination they have done? They were not even ashamed at all; they did not even know how to blush.*
>
> —JEREMIAH 8:12

When I was about ten, I was a regular student in Sunday School of our Presbyterian Church. The class, as I recall, was taught by a prim, deeply religious man who seemed ancient to us, though he was probably in his thirties (he would later go on to try to convert one of the town's few Jewish kids—and fail). We spent a lot of time on the Old Testament, reading scriptures and trying to figure out what they meant. On one particular day, there was a lot about the "circumcised" and the "uncircumcised." It seemed like a pretty big deal. So I asked.

"What is circumcision?"

Boy, did he hesitate. Then he explained, "It's when they cut the skin off your lower finger."

"Lower finger?" I thought. "What could that be?"

On the way out of class, Fred Oxley pulled me aside, "You know, Newkirk, you are a true dumbass. Circumcision is when they cut skin off your dick." I simultaneously winced and felt very stupid.

We can perhaps brush off these moments or convert them to stories, but embarrassment, and our fear of it, plays a powerful role in our lives. I have spent a good part of my life being publicly awkward—or fearing that I would be. I am so self-conscious when I am introduced to someone new, I never remember their name, and have to fake it, sometimes for years. I am ashamed to admit that there was a period when I avoided funerals and memorial services when I could—because I didn't know what to say (only later did I realize that what matters is that you were there and all you had to say is "I'm so sorry").

It is significant that embarrassment only took its current meaning after centuries of use. Its original meaning was something like "barrier" or "obstacle"—an impediment that might be used in a fortification, obviously connected to "barricade." It is this very idea of barrier that will animate this book and that still adheres to the word. We are kept back by our fears of being inadequate, or foolish, or ridiculous. Embarrassment is still a mighty obstacle.

I regularly ask people I work with what the greatest impediment to learning is. It's one of those impossibly large questions, and they normally hesitate a long time to answer, probably annoyed at me. I suspect that they are thinking about some aspect of instruction, or access to instruction, poverty, and racism, something like that. But when I suggest that embarrassment is a likely answer, they usually nod their heads, admitting that it is a least plausible answer. In fact, many of these disadvantages, like racism and poverty, are experienced as ever-present embarrassment or shame—the sense of being an intruder, being unfamiliar with routines that seem second nature to others, fumbling for words and appearing unintelligent.

And for all of us there is some form of learning—dancing, drawing, carpentry—that we would like to try but fear the prospect of being publicly awkward. Unless we can get beyond this reluctance, we never put ourselves out there to learn—we never become the novice we need to be to learn.

So a basic question for educators is: how can we create conditions of support so that students can fail publicly without succumbing to embarrassment, or more likely, finding ways to "hide" so they can protect themselves? A related question is: what allows some students to fail publicly and maintain a healthy sense of competence? My hope is that by naming the enemy—embarrassment—we can make some progress on these questions.

Embarrassment, Shame, and the Rest

Embarrassment is linked to a thesaurus of negative emotions—fear, mortification, self-doubt, regret, humiliation, hesitancy, risk avoidance, chagrin, excessive self-consciousness, and the ever-present imposter complex, that expectation that at any moment we will create the gaffe that exposes us as not belonging. Embarrassment may seem most closely related to shame; it shares that gut feeling of public failure, of not measuring up. But with a crucial difference. Shame would seem to have a moral component. I feel ashamed for being rude, of failing to comfort a friend in distress—in each of these cases I have violated a social ethical norm, and shame is a way society enforces these norms. We can be admonished with, "You should be ashamed" but it would be odd to say, "You should be embarrassed."

Shame, it seems to me, carries with it some intentionality. "I should have known better," we say; there was a code I was responsible for and I violated it. I know if is wrong to be rude—and I was rude. Shame operates in a world where standards are reasonably clear and available, which is why we hold ourselves morally responsible. Logically we shouldn't feel morally responsible for accidents and violations of rules we could not know. But embarrassment isn't logical that way—and the distinction gets messy.

Take the case one of my graduate student, Marino Fernandes, who wrote for a photo memoir about a pair of pants:

> One memory I have about this picture is about the jeans. Every pair of jeans that I see around that period of time reminds me of the one day I needed to go to school but had no clean clothes to do it in. We hadn't had a chance to go to the Laundromat to get it done. I had just learned the word scrub a few weeks earlier. In Portugal it was totally normal for someone to wear the same clothes several days in a row—provided they didn't smell and weren't stained. But I quickly learned that a person who does this in the United States is labeled a "scrub."
>
> So, not having any clean clothes, my brother refused to go to school. It was around 7:00 AM, and my mom was screaming trying to convince my brother to put on some pants and go to school, but he refused.
>
> On the other hand, I had to go to school. That's what I did. That's what I was expected to do. I was the smart one. I was the best English speaker. I was going to school. And I wanted to go. I really did.

So my mom remembered that she had a pair of clean Calvin Klein jeans in her closet and said, with her Portuguese-accented English, "Com'ere let me show you something." And she pulled out these clean CK jeans. "You see, these are Calvin Klein. These are very expensive. Everyone loves Calvin Klein."

That was the first day I had ever heard of Calvin Klein, but I remembered seeing that "CK" all over my friend's clothes. So I took the jeans and went to school.

You can start laughing now.

After the third time I stood up, I learned another thing about jeans: there are women's fit and there are men's fit. A particular subcategory of women's fit jeans is the high-waisted, balloon-assed, taper-ankled mom jeans. And that was what I was wearing. My friend said "Yo, he got girl pants on."

And that is all you need to know about how that went.

His story points to the precarious nature of embarrassment for immigrant students who want to fit in—learning a new set of rules that for native students have become habitual. He and his mother got part of it right (the part about clean clothes each day, the Calvin Klein part) but part wrong (knowing that women's jeans have a different cut, and that it was even more inappropriate to wear them). This incident would seem to be deeply and painfully embarrassing, but not shameful.

But the mystery of embarrassment is that it is so hard to distinguish, emotionally, from shame. What is the moral dimension to being awkward, or publicly inept, if no one is harmed, even offended? Why—if we can distinguish the two emotions like this—do they feel so similar?

A possible answer might be like this—as social beings we feel an obligation to act in a competent way, and perhaps evolution has created emotional mechanisms that sanction us, punish us, when we don't. This appropriateness is not limited to moral behavior; it covers all behavior. It doesn't distinguish. When we are inappropriate, when we commit a gaffe, when we are publicly awkward, we feel for a moment outside of the human collective,

When we are inappropriate, when we commit a gaffe, when we are publicly awkward, we feel for a moment outside of the human collective, stranded, alone.

stranded, alone. Erving Goffman put it this way: that we wear a mask, a "face," and play a role with rules of behavior. When we act inappropriately, not in accordance with the role, the mask momentarily drops and we see our unsocialized face—and it looks like that of a frightened animal.

When I mentioned the accepted distinction between shame and embarrassment to a friend of mine, a professor of English at a prestigious university, he questioned whether they are really so different. He wrote to me:

> Let's say one of my students asks, "Have you read *Paradise Lost* (or *David Copperfield* or *The Sound and the Fury*)? I'd be embarrassed to say no (even though that's the truth), but I might also be ashamed that I haven't read them because I'm an English professor so I feel it's part of my professional obligations but also because I've spent so much of time when I should have been reading them reading the sports pages or surfing the Internet or doing crossword puzzles. My point is that there are some instances of lack of knowledge that seem/feel both embarrassing and shameful.

The embarrassment comes from the public nature of the admission. In other words, we can feel ashamed (in the privacy of our self) without the embarrassment of revealing this information to others. We sometimes withhold information—preferring private shame over public embarrassment—and suffer the psychological consequences.

In the end, it is probably impossible to untangle these two forms of acute discomfort. Even the Oxford English Dictionary (1971) shows only a nuance of difference:

> **Shame:** The painful emotion arising from the consciousness of something dishonouring, ridiculous, or indecorous in one's own conduct or circumstances (or in those of others whose honour or disgrace one regards as one's own), or of being in a situation which offends one's sense of modesty or decency.
>
> **Embarrassment:** Intense emotional or social discomfort caused by an awkward situation or by an awareness that one's own or another's words or actions are inappropriate or compromising, or that they reveal inadequacy or foolishness; awkwardness, self-consciousness.

I suspect that Marino, in his women's-cut Calvin Kleins, could not distinguish between the two forms of social pain—was he compromised or dishonoured (or indecorous)? Was it pain or intense discomfort? Was he awkward or ridiculous?

Does the fact that he simply did not know this convention of dress make it any less shameful (or embarrassing)?

In the end, we are social creatures. As members of a pack, we must perform publicly and when we violate, however unintentionally, any code, we are vulnerable to intense discomfort, which is painful in the moment—and in recollection. And perhaps for this reason, many cultures do not make a linguistic difference between shame and embarrassment (Harris 2006, 531).

When I began writing this book, I was convinced that my focus was on embarrassment, but as I wrote I felt the need to use associated words, denoting what psychologists call the "self-conscious emotions"—regret, shame, performance anxiety, and most importantly a deep-rooted fear of being publicly awkward and inept, of failing in front of others, even if that other, that watcher, is a version of ourselves. So while researchers on this topic feel confident that these terms can and should be distinguished, I will see them as interlocking and sometimes interchangeable. Isn't the fear of performing the anticipation of embarrassment? Doesn't embarrassment, in the moment, easily transmute into shame, even regret—as in the case of the Calvin Klein jeans? Where does one end and the other begin? I will use embarrassment as a primary term that points to this network of self-conscious emotions—an emotional underlife. Although this will be messy at times, I feel it is true to the less compartmentalized emotional reality we all deal with.

In the Spotlight

I am at a masters swim meet at the historic Harvard Blodgett pool. In my sixties I have taken up Masters swimming, often competing in events I swam as a teenager. When you stand on the starting blocks, you can look across to the pool records set by Olympians who swam in the same lanes you are about to swim in—Mary Meagher, Rowdy Gaines. The very starting blocks are exquisitely timed and can let you know, to the one-hundredth of a second, your reaction time after the gun sounds.

This particular meet runs swiftly with as many as thirty heats in each event, and as an older (and slower) swimmer, I am in one of the earlier heats, maybe the tenth, standing behind the block, watching the supposedly slower swimmers compete. Behind me in line are swimmers in the faster heats. You can see the progression of bodies, an inverse aging process, with those near the end of the line sleek and subtly muscled—the body I had so many years ago. But those who go before me look so fast, and my stress level rises as I imagine myself misplaced in too fast a heat. I don't belong here. I even have to watch my balance as I get on the block, maybe getting help from a timer. Why did I come? I'll embarrass myself by lagging behind.

All this drama—and no one is watching. Really. Nothing is riding on my swim. Really. I'm sure my coach will note the time I do, but she never pressures us—she wants us to compete and enjoy the meet. I am creating all of this for myself—I am the engine of my own distress. Even if I did lag behind, misplaced in too fast a heat, no one would care. It happens all the time.

Embarrassment is, in almost all cases, highly disproportionate to the actual perception of others. It is an inverted form of egotism, a false belief that everyone is watching, when in fact we are not at the center of other people's attention. Rather, embarrassment is a distorted mirror, in which we exaggerate the public salience of our performances, imagining that all eyes are on us, when they aren't. This is not to say that we are unnoticed, or not sometimes teased in a painful way. But I suspect that we are often performing for ourselves, and we have internalized a harsh observer, perhaps an amalgam of critical voices from our past. The critic is in our head even when he is not present. This observer is far more attentive and invested than any real spectator, and ready to pick up the smallest imperfection and allow it to overshadow an otherwise adequate performance. A person subject to depression often knows this process in spades.

> Embarrassment is, in almost all cases, highly disproportionate to the actual perception of others. It is an inverted form of egotism, a false belief that everyone is watching, when in fact we are not at the center of other people's attention.

So what I am really addressing is not so much embarrassment itself—but the fear of embarrassment, an often unrealistic fear at that.

Social psychologists call this the "spotlight effect," a very common tendency to overrate the attention others pay to us: "We naively expect that others will be as aware of our missing buttons, cold sores, and bad hair days as we are" (Miller 2007, 254). Embarrassment is termed a "self-conscious" emotion, like pride, humiliation, and shame; we can "see" ourselves (not always accurately) and we can imagine how others see us. From a survival standpoint it is not difficult to imagine the importance of this capacity for social groups. But humans frequently experience distress by imagining an evaluation of their actions that is far more punitive and negative than the actual evaluation.

I recall an incident in college involving a friend of mine, Tom Hammond, who was prone to depression, though we all had little understanding of that illness at the time. I went on a double date with him, which seemed to me to go fine. As we drank our Ohio-allowed 3.2 percent beer, the conversation seemed to flow. Tom was funny as he usually was. But after the date, he berated himself for being boring, just one more sign that he would never get a steady girlfriend. On and on. To continue the story, a few years later I married the woman he dated that night—and I recently asked her about that evening. Was it that bad?

Not at all, she said, "He was a little shy, but so was I. It was Tom Hammond, sweet Tom Hammond."

Risk and Benefit

Why is this tendency to overrate our visibility and exaggerate the negativity of others' reactions so prevalent? Why do so many of us lean that way, being overly self-conscious? In his book, *Thinking, Fast and Slow,* Daniel Kahneman (2011) offers a crucial insight. He cites studies of how we experience loss and gains in different ways, to the point where we often make bad financial decisions because we won't take reasonable risks. Here's an example: suppose I gave you the option of giving you $50 or I would flip a coin and if you called it correctly you would get $150, but if you called it incorrectly, you would get nothing.

From a purely financial point of view, it would be better to take the risk. But holding you back would be the possible regret of missing out on the sure $50—you could walk away with nothing. The loss weighs heavier than the possible gain; it's called "loss aversion." Kahneman writes: "This asymmetry between the power of positive and negative expectations or experiences has an evolutionary history. Organisms that treat threats as more urgent than opportunities have a better chance to survive and reproduce" (2011, 282).

Why is this tendency to overrate our visibility and exaggerate the negativity of others' reactions so prevalent? Why do so many of us lean that way, being overly self-conscious?

This scenario may seem far removed from, say, the decision of a middle school student to raise her hand in a discussion, but the same principle may apply. She is making a gain/loss calculation. If she answers correctly or speaks thoughtfully, she can gain the approval of the teacher, perhaps gratification for her intelligence, and (really perhaps) the admiration of some classmates. If she fumbles, or answers incorrectly, the reaction can be the inverse. The risk is not simply in how she answers: the very act of answering draws attention to one's physical presence—hair, skin, clothes (e.g., Calvin Klein jeans). Let's assume that the positive prospects are equivalent to the negative. According to Kahneman's theory of loss aversion, she may choose not to raise her hand. The possibility of losing something—social standing in the class—could outweigh the gain of answering well.

To put it the other way, excessive self-consciousness may just be a playing out of loss aversion. We own something: social standing, a sense of being a competent member of a community, or even the benefit of being invisible. But as Erving Goffman delights in pointing out, we always operate with the danger of providing discrepant information that undermines our performance of competence. Self-consciousness, even excessive self-consciousness, is very likely an innate predisposition to caution, to not risking the loss of social standing. It is almost as if we are constructed, or many of us are, with an excess capacity for caution, for not standing out.

One question that scholars of loss aversion ask is—at what point will the gain outweigh the loss? When will the gamble be attractive? If, for example, we say that you will win the $150 if you call the coin flip correctly one out of three tries—would that do it? Probably.

I suspect that, in the case of the raised hand, good teachers ask exactly the same kind of question: how can I create conditions so that the possibility of gain so overmatches the possibility of loss that the student raises her hand? If the student knows that a response will be received respectfully, the odds change. You are not completely safe—you never are in any situation—but you are safe enough to take the risk. (In Chapter 4 we will explore ways teachers can change these odds.)

The fact of race, or any cultural bias, also enters in to the risk-benefit equation. Let's say we are in a largely white, affluent university—say Boston College. At the end of a first-year political science class, the professor gives out an assignment and two male students, one white and one African American, have a similar confusion. There is, to be sure, some "risk" in any student asking the professor for a clarification—there is the implication that he or she has not been clear. More significantly there is the question of how this question will be perceived by classmates, who by not asking appear more competent.

The risk is not likely to be felt the same way by the two students. The white student may feel a residual sense of entitlement: he is meant to be there. He was an early admit, not a conditional admit. It feels, well, legitimate, for him to ask the question. He has a reserve of credit to draw on. He can appear confused with little threat to his standing as a student.

By contrast, the African American student may have no such reserve, no history of belonging to this elite university, and since he was conditionally admitted to BC (he had to take summer courses) he feels already on the margins. He is vulnerable to what Claude Steele (2011) calls "stereotype threat." If he is the one to ask for clarification, he will only be reinforcing a perception of marginality, of conditionality. He, perhaps the lone African American in the class, would appear to be the only one who doesn't get the assignment. His action would feed into a perception that he really doesn't belong. It is a far riskier move for him to raise his hand—or ask for any form of help. It can feel deeply embarrassing. It's far easier to muddle through and not ask for help.

Of course, there is nothing preordained here. The instructor could show appreciation for the request to clarify the assignment—perhaps emailing the student to that effect. Or the student could be coached to take this step, putting his own success in the course ahead of any momentary vulnerability.

But when we look at risk-taking in classrooms, students come from different standpoints, different senses of their own "reserves," their accumulated or inherited capital. There is far more than self-will, or grit, at work—there can be deep social threats. Failure may be stimulating and instructive to students with reserves of assurance, but to others it can be threatening and exposing. Again the question for teaching is how we can shift the risk-benefit equation in favor of participation, and how we can remove the stigma, for all students, in seeking help.

It is difficult for white students to imagine the psychological weight of racism and how it too might take a toll. I was reminded of this weight in a recent blog post by Tiffany Martínez (2016), an accomplished undergraduate student at Suffolk University, who received this comment on one of her papers (Figure 2-1).

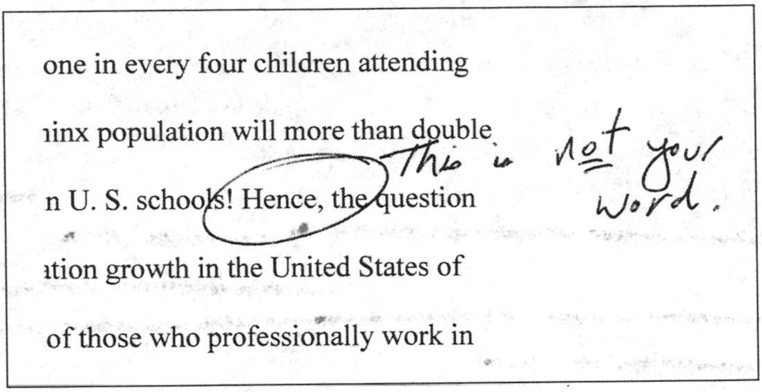

one in every four children attending
ıinx population will more than double
n U. S. schools! Hence, the question
ıtion growth in the United States of
of those who professionally work in

This is not your word.

Figure 2-1

She found this comment (and another accusing her of "cutting and pasting") deeply wounding—why would a professor think that she was not capable of using a linking word like hence? She writes in her blog: "My professor assumed someone like me would never use language like that."

As I read her blog and felt the deep humiliation of the comment, I speculated: "How would a white student respond to a similar comment?" After all it is not uncommon for professors to challenge students on their use of sources, sometimes crudely. I could imagine upset, anger, possibly. But he would not think that professor was classing him in a group ("someone like me"). In fact, he would not even feel that his whiteness placed him in any group (in the same way he would never feel he is stopped for speeding because he is white). The "your" in the comment would be seen, less harmfully, as an individual reference—a mistake. But for Tiffany it invokes a racial stereotype—questioning her very right to even be the student she hopes to be.

Gender also plays a key role in the susceptibility for embarrassment. In *The Second Sex* (1989), Simone de Beauvoir argues that women are acculturated to imagine themselves as the object of the male gaze; they are the focus of attention, the object of attraction, assessed and judged, sensualized and eroticized (i.e., who looks at the men on Oscar night?). The male is the subject, the agent, less visible than the female. According to de Beauvoir, this disparity created a doubleness for women: as objects of attention they have to be more conscious of their appearance, and this self-consciousness undercuts or limits the natural need of women to assert an authentic sense of self—to act in good faith (Bakewell 2016, 214). Theories of "cognitive efficiency" would explain the toll that this heightened visibility can enact. The attention given to awareness of appearance (and anxiety about how one is perceived) distracts from the attention a young woman can give to the task.

Embarrassment in Our Genes (Not Calvin Klein)

We can draw a parallel, I think, between the evolutionary necessity of stress and that of embarrassment. Both serve a survival function, yet in both cases our bodies may be attuned to threats and dangers that have changed with modern conditions for living.

To begin with stress. In his book, *Why Zebras Don't Get Ulcers* (2004), Robert Sapolsky describes the advantages of the stress reaction to acute physical challenges—for example, the imminent attack of a tiger. Energy is released to muscles, your immune system is inhibited (dealing with infections can wait), digestion is slowed—you have better things to do than digest your breakfast, your perception of pain is blunted, aspects of memory and attention improve. In other words, there is an adaptive shift to deal with the crisis.

This biological adaptation, however, works against us if we are in a continual environment of stress—as in an abusive marriage. We become more susceptible to diseases including cancer; we have trouble sleeping; our diet is thrown off—and we can enter a cycle where stress causes us to work poorly with others, and these failures only reinforce the stress we are feeling. Stress interferes with sleep, and our sleeplessness reinforces our stress. The glacial pace of evolution has not matched our changed living conditions, and as a result an important evolutionary adaptation works against us.

Something similar may be at play with our predisposition to embarrassment, particularly when we misjudge and overrate (as I think we regularly do) the negative reception of our embarrassing moment. The question is: are we wired, emotionally, for a previous period of human existence, when bending social norms put the tribe in danger, when individualism and innovation was a threat, when we could hardly be too cautious? In such an environment one could imagine the value of a surplus of inhibition.

The advantage of cooperation and compliance so overbalances the advantages of individual initiative that we became biased to reinforce social norms and to fear stepping beyond them. As Kahneman (2011) suggests, we fear the loss (of social standing and group membership) more than we feel any possible advantages that might come from standing out. The social psychologist Christine Harris elegantly summarizes this conundrum:

> Human beings seem to have an exquisite susceptibility to being manipulated by social situations. We tend to make choices that maintain a veneer of smooth social interaction even while running risks and incurring costs that may be far greater in scope. Embarrassment likely evolved to regulate social behaviors in a way that aids the welfare of the person embarrassed. It often probably does just that, but our intense desire to avoid it may often lead us to engage in rational behaviors that benefit neither ourselves nor those around us. (2006, 533)

As an example, Harris cites the tendency of onlookers to personal tragedies like drownings to delay helping.

Suppose we see someone thrashing in the water—this person may be playing, or may be in serious danger. It would seem that the calculus of risk should tell us to offer help immediately. What's the worst that could happen if you made a mistake? It makes sense to set the threshold low. But if we offer help and it turns out there is no danger, we will be embarrassed—and that caution regularly delays help, so ingrained is the fear of exposing ourselves this way. We also maintain a "veneer of smooth social interaction" when we keep ourselves from voicing disagreements or unpopular viewpoints in meetings—for fear of standing out.

Let me give a very banal example. I was having lunch with my older daughter, then in her twenties, at a local restaurant. It's about 12:30 and the menu clearly states that breakfast won't be served after 11:30. "I feel like an omelet," she says; after all, she had slept late and missed breakfast.

I remind her that the menu clearly states that we are long past time for breakfast.

She waves me off—"I'm sure they can do it." Logically, of course, she was right—they don't send the eggs back to the farm.

Now, to be sure, this is no crisis, but I am still anxious about her request. It feels to me like we are asking for a special privilege, or tampering with the orderly structure of the restaurant. My anxiety comes, as it usually does, from the possibility of a slight disruption of the "situation definition," in this case of the food ordering scenario, where the waitress takes our order and is not put in a position to deny a request (a classic scene in the Jack Nicholson movie *Five Easy Pieces* plays on these conventions). A possible denial is a disruption, a rupture. Embarrassment researchers would call this a "sticky situation" where your actions put someone else in an awkward situation—it creates discomfort on both sides of the request.

When the waitress comes to the table, my daughter engagingly asks, "I know it's lunchtime, but I wonder if I could have one of your bacon and cheese omelets." I wait for the waitress to reinforce the clear rule that was stated in the menu, breakfast time is over. But. Of course. She says, "Sure we can do that."

The Blush

While the thrust of this book will be on how embarrassment undermines learning, it is essential to acknowledge its deep evolutionary roots. According to Robert Sapolsky, we all have basic physiological responses to embarrassing acts:

> This person's body would likely include vasodilation of certain capillary beds and altered sweat gland activity. In other words, the person would blush and get all clammy. Moreover, the person's body movements and facial expressions would change in an unconscious manner—fidgeting, averted gaze, head angled downward and sideways. (2013)

Paradoxically, the appearance of embarrassment assures others that you recognize and submit to the norm you have just violated. These acts work to establish the person's likability and trustworthiness.

Imagine this scene. It is the top of the ninth, and a Red Sox relief pitcher has failed to hold a big lead (not hard to imagine this year, 2015, as I write). A game that seemed a sure win now looks like a sure loss unless the Sox have a big bottom of the ninth. The manager goes to the mound, there is the ritual handing over of the ball. And the walk to the dugout.

It is this walk, the way it is done, that I want to explore. The crowd of 35,000 fans expects a certain kind of walk, one that acknowledges the disaster that has just occurred. We expect a somber expression, a lowering of the head—the pitcher should be looking at the ground, not at us. And although we won't be able to pick up this detail, his head will most likely be tilted toward the left (Harris 2006, 529). He should walk slowly, as if meditating on what has happened. If these rules are violated—if, for example, he walks off with his head erect, or smiling, or if he does something like twirl his glove, or trot off—we, as fans, feel disrespected. We want some acknowledgment of what has happened.

At times like this we are solidly in the animal kingdom, the herd, where acts of submission are essential for maintaining group cohesion. Acts like the pitcher lowering his head serves the function, the absolutely crucial function, of allowing him to stay within the fold, to remain a member in good standing in the Red Sox herd. He symbolically and gesturally expresses regret, takes responsibility, and we as viewers can expect him to work on whatever caused the problem.

Of course, the most evident—and involuntary—manifestation of embarrassment is the blush, about which there is a long history and even body of research. Here is one of the most compelling and eloquent descriptions of the function of blushing:

> Those who are blushing are somehow saying that they know, care about and fear others' evaluations and that they share those values deeply; they also communicate their sorrow over any possible faults or inadequacies on their part, thus performing an acknowledgement, and an apology aimed at inhibiting others' aggression or avoiding social ostracism. (Castelfranchi and Poggi 1990, 240)

The inability to blush was considered by the Biblical prophet Jeremiah as evidence of moral depravity.

A predisposition to caution also seems to work in our memories—at least mine. I have always been puzzled that my embarrassing memories of moments, often small ones, are as acute, or more acute, than memories of major positive events. And I seem, involuntarily, to revisit them more often. A rude remark to my dad a half century ago, for example—it seems freakish and, yes, embarrassing to admit.

But when I broached this tendency with David Pillemer, an expert in episodic memory, he claimed it was perfectly natural. Episodic memory, he explained, is "failure driven," and for good survival reasons. "When things go wrong, it is in our interests to hold on to the memory, so that we don't make the same mistake next time." (See also Schank 1980.) But when a memory of a rude comment, spoken fifty years ago, floats back to me on a sleepless night, I suspect I suffer from an evolutionary surplus that exceeds any pragmatic value.

* * * *

Mercifully my time to swim arrives, the gun goes off, and once in the water my body takes over. I get into a rhythm and manage all the flip turns, I touch the timing pad on the wall, look up to see my time, and it's about what I expected, what I predicted. I wait until the following heat dives in, swim to the side and leave the pool. I am not embarrassed, I am relieved. But then, it was never a real possibility anyway—because no one was watching. Only me. I'm fascinated by this disconnect.

There is a perverse egotism in all this, a grandiosity, to think that as a sixty-seven-year-old swimmer, I am so attended to. An utter lack of realism—and I know that in this setting I may, ultimately, be safe (after all I swam as a kid and am fairly good at it). But there are whole regions of skills I would like to learn but hold back for fear of embarrassment. Dancing is one. Dog training is another. Open water swimming in the ocean is another. I wonder what it must be like for a struggling third grader to read aloud, or an overweight sixth grader to run the mandatory timed mile. Are we all in this damn fraternity of embarrassment? Do we never escape the insecure thirteen-year-old we had hoped to outgrow?

I am convinced, absolutely convinced, that embarrassment is not only a true enemy of learning, but of so many other actions we could take to better ourselves. I recently was talking to a local physician about this idea (no one is safe when I am obsessed with something)—and he noted that embarrassment plays a huge role in seeking health care. We are all embarrassed by the malfunctioning of our bodies—and to seek help is to expose our vulnerability and frailty. Yet our doctors need to know this and are rarely (in my experience) judgmental. They deal with frailty.

I am convinced, absolutely convinced, that embarrassment is not only a true enemy of learning, but of so many other actions we could take to better ourselves.

In this book, we will spend time with students and hear them describe this enemy. We will talk to coaches and athletes who often fail, very publicly, to see how they cope with it, how they maintain a positive attitude in the face of public difficulty. And we will enter the world of special education and English language learning—to see how teachers and students navigate the landscape of stigma, of being marked as different, identified as needing "special" help.

This topic affects us all—as teachers, as students, as participants in public life. None of us escapes the fear of performing poorly, ineptly, in public. All of us have done it at some point. We all deal—successfully or not—with the fear of being seen as incompetent, even if the only person who sees this is . . . ourselves.

So let's do battle, name and identify the enemy that can haunt our days, disturb our sleep, put barriers up to learning, and drain joy from our lives—and maybe we can also learn how to rearrange some things in our own head so that we can be more generous toward ourselves. While embarrassment is only partly about our relationships to others, I am convinced it is primarily about how we relate to ourselves, about the voices in our head that we listen to.

While embarrassment is only partly about our relationships to others, I am convinced it is primarily about how we relate to ourselves, about the voices in our head that we listen to.

(CHAPTER 3)

Stigma

It's just laziness that makes people classify themselves according to appearances, and fail to find anything in common.

—DOSTOEVSKY, *THE IDIOT*

In the last scene of *Midsummer's Night's Dream,* as all the proper lovers are reunited, and after Titania is no longer enamored of an ass, she proclaims a blessing on all: that "all the couples three/ever true in loving be." And that the children they bear should be free of imperfections:

> And the blots of Nature's hand
> Shall not in their issue stand—
> Never mole, harelip, nor scar,
> Nor mark prodigious, such as are
> Despised in nativity. (act V, scene 1)

What strikes me about this wish is the assumption that these imperfections are inevitably "despised"—that this is an inescapable feature of human prejudice.

This mark of difference, whether it be biological (a birthmark) or social (a "scarlet letter"), marks the possessor as different and set apart. It's a stigma—the archaic root is the mark made by a pointed stick, or in medicine "a place or point on the skin that bleeds during certain mental states, as in hysteria." We now use *stigma* less literally, yet still some students are inescapably *marked*: at some point in the school day they may leave the "regular" classroom to get special help. Aeriale, who was labeled "slow learning disabled," described her stigma:

> The most embarrassing part of being labeled an SLD student was being singled out and at times isolated. I remember during tests in grade school I would have to move from my desk next to my teacher so she could help me when needed. I'm grateful for the extra help that I was provided but the toll it took on my self-esteem wasn't worth it. In seventh grade I was placed in a special class with one teacher and I didn't change classes like all the other students in school. Kids are mean but they are mean because they don't understand that it's ok to be different. For whatever reason we have a fear of anything different, so they picked on me, a few called me names, pointed fingers, and thought I was stupid but I wasn't, I just learned differently. It might not seem like a big deal but when a child is already struggling to feel normal and you interrupt their normal routine, you make them feel different and being different is seen as something negative. Therefore they see their selves in a negative light.

These are the "sped" kids. Or they may be the students learning English as a second or third or fourth language—who may be consigned to classes in the basement or trailer.

Even the language of disability, including the word *disability* itself, is continually evolving as certain terms take on negative associations. For example, the term *retarded*, literally "slowed," which came into fashion around the 1920s, might be seen as even more positive than the current "learning disabled" or Aeriale's cruel label "slow learning disabled"—but it is soiled by its association with the "scientific" levels of retardation (in ascending order: imbecile, idiot, and moron). These terms have, mercifully, been erased from scientific diagnosis, though not from the playground taunt. One can easily imagine a relatively short shelf life for "slow learning disabled," which I would predict will give way to a new label that will in turn accumulate negative connotations. We inadvertently acknowledge stigma when we seek for euphemisms to describe certain conditions, for example "sight challenged" for partially blind.

How do students marked as different build a positive learning identity? How do they learn to leave their peers for special help with their head held high? Unembarrassed.

In this chapter we will enter this world of stigma and difference. How do students marked as different build a positive learning identity? How do they learn to leave their peers for special help with their head held high? Unembarrassed. If we are looking for profiles in courage, this might be a good place to look.

Schools face what might be called the paradox of offering help—and well-intentioned efforts to help can be resisted. To offer help to a group (free lunch students, English as a Second Language [ESL] students, special needs students), you need a designation for that group, and that very designation may be so stigmatizing that students would rather forgo the help than to accept the label. My colleague Christina Ortmeier-Hooper (2008) documents this resistance in her essay, "English May Be My Second Language, but I'm Not 'ESL.'" Students may choose to camouflage their linguistic or cultural background—their designation as an ESL student—so as not to appear too different.

She quotes from an interview with Jane (pseudonym), a college student who describes the stigma of the ESL designation in middle school:

> You feel like you are behind everyone else. That you are not maybe as intelligent. Which is not true at all. But you feel very behind. I feel like the ESL program is very isolating. They have their own little room that you have to go to. At that age (junior high), it can really hurt a teen . . . an adolescent's self-esteem. (409)

I asked Christina about how schools either create or diffuse this sense of stigma—and she mentioned that the geography of assistance is extremely important. Is the place of help an isolated and marginal space (a trailer, a basement) or is it integrated into the main area of the school? How long is the walk they must take, how exposed? When Jane speaks of "their own little room" she seems to be supporting this notion: that simply being assigned to *that space*, to be segregated in that way, works to stigmatize.

The geography of assistance is extremely important. Is the place of help an isolated and marginal space (a trailer, a basement) or is it integrated into the main area of the school? How long is the walk they must take, how exposed?

Recent research confirms that students may be right in resisting the ELL/EL (English learner) label. A study conducted by Ilana Umansky (2016) found that students "on the cusp" of being able to function in mainstream classes—who were identified as EL in kindergarten—scored lower than their nonidentified counterparts later in school in math and English language arts. Umansky attributes this result to lower teacher expectations and the stigma of the label.

Even without a label, ELLs often feel their difference. They are the "quiet ones." I have found this particularly to be the case for ELLs who find it hard to enter the flow of conversation. It moves too fast. Forced to choose between two forms of embarrassment—an ill-formed or poorly timed contribution to the discussion, or silence—the choice is clear. One of my graduate students memorably describes her difficulties in a seminar:

> I am the silent one and usually take the last-minute turn to speak with the guts I have cumulated from the first minute of the class. My statement sounds like the ending song of a movie—being supposed to sound beautiful but usually ending being powerless to attract most of the audience who are about to leave the theater. Over time, I have gotten used to being away from the attention center. It happens. When you keep silent, people around you would not feel your presence. I therefore define myself as a silent person in the seminar: "Hi, I'm that silent one in class."

The silence is embarrassing, humiliating. She goes on with another metaphor for her situation:

> Maybe it is more precise to describe me as a duck in a rapid river full of whirlpools. The duck swims quietly and peacefully in the golden pond, but can never enjoy herself when drawn into the rapid river, not to mention when swallowed by whirlpools. Her life is no longer in her hands but in the whirlpools. She has no idea how deep the whirlpool will absorb her down into, when the whirlpool will spit her out and send her to the smooth stream, whether she will have a chance to stretch her neck to take a deep breath and utter two "quack, quacks" before she is swallowed into a new whirlpool.

This is the antithesis of finding voice; it is the desperate image of drowning in the rapid exchange of language, the whirlpool. The question is how can we create the "golden pond" where she can function.

The closest I have been to an ELL was the time I spent in France, trying to retrieve language deposited in the dendrites of my brain decades ago. It wasn't pretty. Often my attempts at communication were met by blank stares, and often a decision that the listener's English was better than my French, so we switched to English. And if there was much French for me to process, I experienced what Brian Tomlinson called "language waterboarding": "sentences piled on top of sentences, each layer diminishing my already-shaky receptive capacity" (Tomlinson 2016). That was me a lot of the time.

But I could manage to shop and ask directions, and even have minimal conversations—*if I could plan what I was going to say.* And it felt exhilarating when I could do this. Going into a shop I would rehearse my vocabulary of amounts and kinds of food, so I would be ready to talk. It felt wonderful to be able to manage these simple transactions in another language.

Everyone In

I have found that this same principle can help the student who finds the whirlpool of classroom discussion hard to enter. It is so much better if you have a guaranteed turn—and you know when it will happen. The student doesn't have to bid for recognition and can plan what he or she will say. One technique that I like is the *sweep.* Suppose everyone in the class has been freewriting on a topic like food (favorite restaurants, holiday meals, candy—a great topic really). I might after the freewrite swing around the class and ask each student to say, in a couple of sentences, what they have written about. We follow the seating order, so everyone knows when they will contribute, and such a short contribution is relatively low risk. It takes only a few minutes, but in that time we all hear the full range of topics—and everyone speaks. I hear every voice, even the "quiet" ones.

The very *act of writing* can also serve as a form of rehearsal. If, for example, we want to see how students imagine a character in a story, I can throw that question out to the class—favoring the more spontaneous and confident students. Or I could ask each student to write words that may describe the character (*mean, kind, obnoxious*) and attach to one of these words a detail that causes the student to think that way. This practice reinforces the fundamental practice of providing evidence for a claim—and it is essential at all levels of reading. Knowing that students have done that writing, I can be more assured that I can draw them in. It's a low threshold—they can simply read what they have written. A variation on this practice is to have students *turn and talk* before entering into a class discussion.

To sum up, traditional classroom talk is based on an opt-in approach. Students choose (or refuse) to enter in; they bid for a turn by raising their hands and being recognized. But if turns are guaranteed and predictable, discussion can shift to an opt-out approach—that is, students are automatically *in*, unless they choose not to speak. If a desired form of activity—be it investing regularly, or dental checkups, or getting help with our writing—is the default position (one we do not have to choose), we are far more likely to engage in it. These practices can benefit not only ELLs but any student who feels uncomfortable or unable to enter the swift stream of discussion. Even these scheduled turns can be stressful—so I try in every way I can, through my voice and posture, to slow time, to help the student feel there is no rush.

In the area of writing, ELL students can be assisted in using their various literacies and cultural loyalties—again a practice called a "permeable curriculum" (Dyson 2016)—that can benefit all students. A permeable curriculum allows the outside in; it recognizes that there can be a profitable interaction between school goals and the outside passions of students—indeed the outside becomes the engine for the inside. The British linguist Basil Bernstein declared this inclusiveness a moral imperative:

> If the culture of the teacher is to become part of the consciousness of the child, then the culture of the child must first become part of the consciousness of the teacher. . . . We should start to realize that the social experience the child already possesses is valid and significant and that this social experience should be reflected back to him as valid and significant. It can only be reflected back to him if it is part of the texture of the learning experience we create. (1970, 57–58)

But the question for writing teachers is how to do that—how exactly can this "outside" be used?

In a memorable image, Christina Ortmeier-Hooper describes a curious paralysis when it comes to the cultural and linguistic resources of ELL students:

> But sometimes the cultural fabric can feel like it only has aesthetic merit, like a beautiful tapestry that hangs on a museum wall. In the museum we often admire the weaving of the cloth and images, but we fail to remember that the tapestry served another functional purpose, warming and insulating the cold interior walls of ancient stone castles. In a similar fashion we admire the multicultural backgrounds that our students bring

> to the classroom, but we do not always see the functional aspects of their backgrounds particularly in terms of writing. (2013, 94)

In her book, *The ELL Writer,* she describes the way she works with ELL students to create literacy maps upon which they place their names at the center, and then spreading out from it they paste cut pieces of construction paper. On each piece they name some part of their literacy world—experiences in their home country, song lyrics, children's books they remember, websites they visit, favorite performers or singers, sports loyalties, fan fiction they might write, and so on. Echoing the great literacy ethnographer Shirley Brice Heath, Ortmeier-Hooper demonstrates that even students who struggle with school literacy often participate in rich literate environments—and that this participation can provide content and topics for school writing. If, for example, a school goal is to make claims and provide evidence, why not evaluate a new video game, or the most recent Harry Potter book, or the Red Sox pitching rotation. The outside meets the inside.

Locating these sources of strength is the one indispensable principle in writing instruction, illustrated in a *New Yorker* cartoon that my mentor Don Murray had pinned to his bulletin board. A man is seated at a typewriter on his porch, pipe in mouth, armed crossed, obviously experiencing writer's block. He is surrounded by dogs—they peer out of every window, they surround him—mutts, hounds, terriers, bulldogs, a lumbering lab. There is a litter of puppies on the porch and a picture of a favorite dog hung on the wall.

Standing in the doorway of the porch is his wife, who offers this advice— "Write about dogs."

Labels and Stigma

Clearly, those who work with these identified groups must be adept at defusing this sense of differentness—being sensitive about labels, for example. I recall during my visits to British schools that one had a tracking system: students were assigned to the X, Y, or Z tracks—and in England, the Z is pronounced "zed." Students in the lowest track became the "zeds."

Here is how Aeriale described her six-year experience as a labeled student:

> I would like to share my story with you. As a child I was labeled an SLD [slow learning disabilities] student. My earliest memory of this was in third grade. Each week I would attend a special group with other kids that shared this label.

> It was also the year a test called SSAT would measure my knowledge. This will mark the moment I realized I was different. It will also be the moment I learned I didn't have to allow anyone to define me or my learning capabilities. I was pulled from my class and forced to take this major test in a strange classroom with teachers and students I did not know. I can still remember the confusion, feel the stress and shame. I can remember feeling singled out.
>
> This was a weeklong test and that Monday I hated school for the first time and with tear-filled eyes I took my test. The next morning I told my teacher that I did not want to go to the other class. That I wanted to stay in her class with my friends. She responded "I didn't have a choice." It wasn't up to her, and that I had to go and take the test where I could receive extra attention. I remember getting to the SLD classroom and being so upset. Feeling like I did something wrong. Like I failed, that I was stupid.

Tests, and testing situations, would continue to define her: in twelfth grade, she performed so low on a standardized test that she was advised to go into "nail tech" because of her low reading and math scores—a future she and her parents rejected. Aeriale became what Pam Mueller has called a "lifer," caught in a system that defined her and that she could not exit, at least for six years.

> The feelings of shame and unworthiness would consume me. I was already a shy and quiet child but now I would walk with my head down in embarrassment for the next six years. Embarrassment I shouldn't of had. I was labeled with a disability and the school system would take every opportunity to help me by putting me in classes that did not help me but simply passed me onto the next grade. If I'm being honest, it was as if they wanted to label me. That they wanted me to feel like I wasn't normal, that I couldn't do what everyone else could so why try.

In the end her story is a happy one: with the help of some of her teachers she was able to define her own learning style, and, as she says, not define herself in terms of her disability, though she admits she still hears a "small weak voice" telling her: "You can't, you aren't able, you have a learning disability, just accept it and settle." She adds, "Now I live to prove that voice wrong."

A radical difference in learning materials can also mark the student as part of a stigmatized group. A colleague of mine tells the story of a book assigned to her middle school son—*My Pet Dick* (Colleta 1979). It's a title that positively begs for a comma. The book is a small children's paperback, clearly written for primary age children, with a smiling duck (named Dick) on the cover. It has a reading level (13) clearly marked. Apparently his special ed teacher thought the book would be a good resource for teaching short vowels.

When she dug the book out of his backpack, my friend was outraged that her son—who even at that age was helping with a small family business—would be given such an infantile book? One can easily imagine the embarrassment that might come from peers seeing the book, and the potential for bullying. It would mark him as someone dramatically behind his peers in reading. It would mark him as clueless concerning the careless sexual connotation of the title. It could make him a target.

The classic, and at times brutally realistic, work on stigma is Erving Goffman's *Stigma: Notes on the Management of Spoiled Identity* (1963). In it he offers a set of terms that might be useful in describing situations like the ones above. As noted earlier, Goffman sees all social behavior as *performance:* we are always on stage, in a situation, and we and others hold ourselves to a set of expected performative rules (as husband, teacher, student, and so on).

A key to being seen as a competent performer is the *control of information*—to reveal only those traits that conform to the ideal we aspire to. We damage our performance with *slips,* or instances when we fail to monitor behavior that undercuts our desired performance. Goffman writes: "We must be prepared to see that the impression of reality fostered by a performance is a delicate, fragile thing that can be shattered by a very minor mishap" (1963, 56).

As an example, in one of the 1992 presidential debates, George H. Bush looked down at his watch. It is the one lasting image from the debate. While it is understandable that someone in his position would want to know the time, it gave the impression that he was anxious for the debate to be over—this undercut a performative expectation that he completely welcomes the chance to speak to voters (his opponent, Bill Clinton clearly got that right!). In the same way, allowing classmates to see *My Pet Dick* would have been a lapse of informational management, undercutting this young man's desire to be viewed as a normal student.

A central term for Goffman is *identity,* not simply what we might think of ourselves, but the categorization that others make of us, often when one trait (or perhaps stigmatized attribute) stands in for the whole person. Most of us have experienced something like this when we've had a very visible injury like a broken leg in a cast—it becomes the invariable, and ultimately tedious, topic of conversation. We *are* our injury, at least for a time. Skin color, sexual orientation, occupation, criminal record, disability, immigration status—all lead to convenient categorization. Assigning a singular identity, a form of stereotyping, is a way of creating cognitive ease.

Stereotyping helps us avoid the messy and demanding challenge of opening ourselves to others, to their diverse and unexpected traits—and not incidentally it reinforces our own sense of superiority. Students may prefer to be recognized for mainstream acculturated traits (love of fan fiction, being a lacrosse player) than their linguistic difference that sets them apart. Claude Steele, whom I have cited earlier, tells of a strategy that one of his male African American grad students used when out at night. Aware that he might appear threatening, he whistles Vivaldi to disrupt the identity that might be assigned to him.

One key strategy for someone with a potentially stigmatizing characteristic is *passing*. This is a term originally used to describe how light-skinned African Americans passed for Caucasian. Goffman uses it to describe any act to disguise a sign of difference. We see this all the time among struggling readers. In a class where they feel themselves well behind, they may "fake read"; they will pick books well above their reading level and turn the pages, appearing little different than their classmates. Another strategy is to move a bookmark ahead in a book you are not really reading. We similarly try to pass by simply pretending to understand things we don't (a near permanent condition for me in math classes).

Aeriale describes this scenario where a teacher helped her "pass" during oral reading sessions:

> Reading out loud was my worse fear. I was so ashamed that I couldn't read like everyone else. That I couldn't pronounce the words even though I knew them. My fifth-grade teacher never made me read out loud to the class. Instead of going down the row, she would skip around, never calling on me. This is the only time a teacher would go out of their way to not make it obvious that I wasn't being called on to read. In middle and high school the teachers would call students row by row to read and just skip over me. My stomach was always in knots on these days.

In other words, the teacher protected Aeriale, allowed her to appear normal—she just wasn't called on. But if this strategy became apparent to other students, there would be a failure of information control.

One of the most common strategies for passing is remaining silent, not volunteering an answer, not risking exposure. This strategy is widely reported by individuals with hearing impairments (Jaworski and Stephens 1998; Nora 2007) and ELLs. In a classroom, group silence can allow the student to feel part of the solidarity of the group, even when confused or uncomprehending of the material being presented. The strategy is especially effective if accompanied by an expression of attentiveness, a steady forward focus—all of which grants the status of being a student in good standing.

Goffman actually uses the term *face* (as in "saving face") to describe this sense of feeling and being perceived as a competent and respected member of a group. The term originated in China, where there are many variants. According to Lin Yutang, face is "the most delicate standard by which Chinese social intercourse is regulated" (1935, 199–200). The term is typically used metaphorically. But when we "lose face," for example, fail to answer a question, there is often the dropping of the mask of competence, and there is the actual look of panic, as if we have momentarily lost our status.

In the traditional recitation, IRE (initiate-response-evaluation) format, silence is not a guaranteed right—because the rules of the game allow the teacher to ask students with unraised hands to answer a question. But any teacher with an ounce of social intelligence knows the risk. The blush. The startled look, the hesitancy. The searching for words. The fear on our part that this action that we hoped would draw a silent student out, maybe be a breakthrough, will in fact only drive her further into silence.

Julie Nora transcribed an example of "face-losing" in a middle school social studies classroom where all students were ELL. The format of the class followed the IRE model, but as often happens, no one bid to answer questions—which led to this painful moment for Marco, who never raised his hand:

> Mr. C: What is the Constitution? (no hands) What is the Constitution? Oh my God. (some hands) What is the Constitution? Marco.
>
> (Students laugh)
>
> Mr. C: What are we studying now? What is the Constitution? Marco? (whistles) Marco, we did this whole big project, we cut out these big letters, "We the people of the United States, in order to form a more perfect union . . ." This is the Preamble to the Constitution. The Constitution that was written in Philadelphia. That we've been studying. What is it? In your own words? What is the Constitution? Marco, maybe you can get your history book.

(Marco is silent)

(Students laugh)

(Marco gets up)

Mr. C: See Juan, Juan will help you.

Lisa: He playing with him. (Nora 2007, 84)

It is not surprising that no one would bid to answer such a nebulous question as "What is the Constitution"—in your own words. The intent here is clearly intentional embarrassment, humiliation. Marco pays the triple penalty of being singled out, of continuing to remain silent, and of having to receive "help" from Juan, all to the laughter of classmates.

Passing, to be sure, is not a strategy limited to those with a socially defined stigma. As Goffman sees it, it is a basic demand of performance. There are *idealized* standards we attempt to meet to be fully credible—yet there are traits, attitudes, shortcomings that if made public would undermine that performance. We all live with the demand for information management and the alarming possibility that we will reveal discrepant information that will cause us to *lose face* and even reveal us as *imposters*. If I were to admit that I find *Hamlet* a boring play (which I do—too long, and he is such a jerk to Ophelia), that admission might undercut my credibility among my English department colleagues. But didn't I quote Shakespeare to start this chapter? Do I pass?

Prejudice and rigid stereotyping feed on exclusion and lack of contact. Familiarity undercuts this.

The vast effort in this country to mainstream and include disabilities in the classroom might well be seen as destigmatizing. To be sure, there are educational advantages (and some disadvantages) to this process, but a clear effect is to make disabilities seem normal, part of a natural human continuum. Prejudice and rigid stereotyping feed on exclusion and lack of contact. Familiarity undercuts this.

Still, even in an inclusive class it is evident to all students which students have child-specific aides—who in Goffman's terms "mark the student." Aides are, of course, aware of this and some that I have spoken with develop strategies for *covering*, or making less overt, their assignment to an individual student. They may do this by providing help to other, nonidentified students, acting more as a general classroom aide, while still attending to the student they have special responsibility for. But the child who spends a good part of the day with an aide hovering above him and around him pays a social price, no matter the value of the assistance given.

Common Ground

All my career, I have been reluctant to even express an opinion about special education. The work is so entailed with labels, testing, legalities, complex obligations, and plans. I had seen my wife work with children with severe emotional disabilities—where physical restraint was always a concern. Though like most teachers I have taught troubled and struggling students, I never wanted to offer glib solutions concerning situations I have never experienced.

Yet in speaking with Andrea Rousso, a special educator with long and varied experience in the New York City schools, and other special educators, I began to feel common ground. Much of what I learned took me back to a mantra of Donald Graves, who when observing a child, would always ask, "What *can* she do?" He was not focused on the deficits, but on the competencies. For example, a child "misspelling" a word is usually getting most of it right, usually the consonants that shape pronunciation. A child "pretend reading" a book often has the storytelling voice, a sense of starting at the beginning of the book and moving to the end, and a command of the left-to-right/top-to-bottom directionality of print. It all brought to mind the great "observers" or kidwatchers of the 1980s—Jerome Harste, Yetta Goodman, Marie Clay—and their spiritual heirs Irene Fountas, Gay Sue Pinnell, Katie Ray, Matt Glover, and Kathy Collins.

In Rousso's view, the heart of special education is built around three questions—"What do I see? What do I think? What might I try?"—and then including the student in the process: "Instead of saying, 'How can I get this kid up to speed?' I need to ask, 'What is happening?' I might say, 'It takes you a long time to figure out how to spell words. Is that what you notice?' 'Great. Then let's see what we can do about it.'"

Central to this approach is the capacity to notice what might be called *microimprovements*:

> Diagnostic prescriptive teaching involves looking at the minutiae of the learning, the subtleties, and being able to recognize that there are small

> gains even though they are not the gains the teacher needs to see or even though they might not be measurable. There are subtle ways kids move forward that people don't always see.

A small change might be something like being more patient in solving a hard problem and not becoming instantly frustrated. Her approach echoes the advice of Peter Johnston (2004) who claims that as we help students notice these subtle improvements and give them names, we create a narrative of progress.

Rousso explained a strategy called "demystification," which is embedded in the work of Dr. Mel Levine, and involves moving beyond the more global labels like attention deficit disorder or attention deficit hyperactivity disorder:

> The more we can understand the specificity of what students are experiencing the better the instruction. Because then you can isolate the weakness or problem rather than defining their whole self by that weakness. If the student is struggling with math, it's not a math weakness, it's maybe a weakness in remembering the math facts, or maybe a weakness in lining up your numbers. You get very specific and the teacher and student become aligned on those specific parts of the larger subject.

Noted special educator Rick Lavoie (2002) considers demystification a central strategy in removing the global stigma of learning disability:

> If you have a child with diabetes, one of the first things you do is explain to the child, "This is what diabetes is, these are the foods you can eat, this is what's happening to your body when you don't eat the proper food," and explain line and verse.
>
> Yet when a child has a learning problem, we try to protect the child from it. I've had parents say to me, "He doesn't know he has a learning problem." Indeed he does. And sometimes the child takes great comfort in the diagnosis, in knowing "I'm not the only person that has it, I'm not stupid like the kids tell me in the school bus. I'm not lazy." (PBS 2002)

The benefits of this clinical and analytic approach to difficulty—and the movement away from global explanations—will be a theme of this book. As I understand demystification, it sounds very much like Rich Kent (whom we will meet later) helping his athletes become "students of the game." Rousso's students, as they become "aligned" for instruction, become students of the game—the game being their own learning processes. They gain analytic tools and language to replace their global designation. Of course, developing the observational tools of diagnosis and the practical repertoire of work-around strategies is the task of a lifetime, not of any one book or obviously one short chapter. But to those of us raised on observational practices of kidwatching, it feels familiar.

One common way of enacting this positive approach is to adopt Howard Gardner's notion of *multiple intelligences*: that children who struggle, for example with print, may have social or artistic or kinesthetic modalities that are true strengths. It makes little sense, when dealing with a struggling reader, to simply double down on the work that is giving difficulty, ignoring areas of strength.

A good first step is to open schooling up to a wider range of competencies. For example, my colleague Tomasen Carey believed that joke telling could provide a good stage for some of her students, so she regularly scheduled a time of day for that (with some judicious guidelines, and the expectation that performers would practice their jokes in small groups).

Rousso calls this process of locating strengths "finding the student" and recalled one of her special education students, a sixth grader who was a virtual nonreader, breaking down at about 11:00 every day. But he had an impressive memory. She gave him the job of beginning the day by reviewing in detail what had happened the previous day. In doing so he "created an image of himself that was valuable to him and his classmates," which reduced the occasions for breaking down and acting out. Psychologist Michael Thompson claims that the great developmental necessity of the middle school years is to discover an area of competency. Self-esteem cannot be built upon wind or empty assurances—it requires objective and publicly acknowledged demonstrations of competence; being good at something (PBS 2006).

Yet at the same time it is irresponsible to ignore the areas that need work, that count for school success, and dwell solely in the more comfortable modalities. The question, it seems to me, is how the stronger areas can pull along and support the weaker areas. It is the interaction of intelligences. The metaphor that comes to mind is *drafting*. This is a term used in car racing and cycling, or less often in swimming and running. In the Tour de France the lead cyclist breaks the wind, creating a kind of pocket for those who follow—the leader must expend more energy but also pulls followers along.

Figure 3-1

In the same way, the learner who usually has stronger systems can draft weaker systems. For example, it is very common for a young writer, often a boy, who struggles with print to be a good drawer (Figure 3-1).

For first-grader Noah, drawing is far more engaging, and his cartoon style was popular and widely admired by classmates. Building on the drawing, the student can be urged to write speech bubbles, captions, titles—words. Unfortunately, in too many cases, the message is "let's focus on the writing and stop wasting time with the drawing." In other words, we need to treat writing as multimodal, involving multiple systems—drama and performance, drawing, writing—that mutually support each other.

This drafting can work in other ways. When I think of what pulls writers along, the perhaps obvious answer is the opportunity to dwell in subjects of interest, what might be called "identity themes." An identity theme is something more than an interest; it is a central passion and competence, the way we might complete the sentence, "I am a ________________."

Not many students would put *writer* in that blank, but they might put painter, or soccer player, or video geek, or Star Wars fanatic, or joke teller, or assistant manager at Panera. And it is my job as a teacher to learn these identity themes and to help them build writing projects around them. We have to be curious and know our students. Writing (and reading) then can become not some neutral isolated "skill" but a way of participating in a passion—of rendering it, recalling it, analyzing it, sharing it. Writing piggybacks onto identity. Which may be a fancy way of saying, "Write about dogs."

We All Need a Sidekick

Ron Suskind, a writer for the *Wall Street Journal*, illustrated this drafting principle in his incredibly moving account of his severely autistic son. Owen developed normally until age three, at which point he closed down totally; he fell silent, wouldn't make eye contact, and would only say the single word: *juice*. The psychologists Suskind and his wife consulted diagnosed "regressive autism." The only joint family activity was watching Disney movies, endlessly and repetitively. In one hopeful moment, they realized that Owen's "juice" was really from a line in *The Little Mermaid*: "It won't cost much, just your voice." But even so, the specialists discounted this repetition as *echolalia*, mere repeating common among autistic children—no big breakthrough, after all.

As it turns out, Owen's obsession with Disney was his way back, his lifeline. At age six and a half, on his brother Walter's ninth birthday, Owen emerged from his silence and commented on his brother's sadness at his own party: "Walter doesn't want to grow up, like Mowgli or Peter Pan." Suskind writes:

> It's as if Owen had let us in, just for an instant, to glimpse the mysterious grid growing inside him, a matrix on which he affixed items he saw each day that we might not even notice. And then he carefully aligned it to another one, standing parallel: The World of Disney. (Suskind 2014)

His parents, desperate to find a way into that matrix, began to communicate with Owen by impersonating Disney characters. Suskind *became* Iago from *Aladdin* or Baloo from *The Jungle Book* ("Look for the bare necessities . . .").

Owen developed a special connection with sidekicks, often some of Disney's most vivid and interesting characters—Jiminy Cricket in *Pinocchio*, Zazu and Rafiki in *The Lion King*. The sidekick is invariably loyal, often a good counselor, a reassuring voice, someone who can keep the hero focused on his mission—in Owen's words, "A sidekick helps a hero fulfill his destiny. I am one. I am a sidekick."

By attending obsessively to sidekicks in Disney movies, internalizing the kinds of advice they gave, Owen could give himself advice on how to act, how to become a friend:

> Owen has been whispering under his breath to sidekicks for years, having them guide him as he faces challenges. He is developing a version of "inner speech," something that typical people develop as

> children think through: behavior and plan actions, the core cognitive practices of executive function, which are often thought to be deficient in autistic people. Lately, Owen has let us in on it. At our prompting, he tells us how various sidekicks would solve his problems, quell his fears. (Suskind 2014)

In reading this moving account of Owen and his sidekicks, it occurred to me that a central task of special educators, all educators really, is to help learners develop their own sidekicks, internal voices that can counteract stigma and the cultural message that they are deficient. That can tell a different story. This "voice" has been given a number of names: monitor, metacognitive awareness, conscience, other self, secret sharer, doppelganger. Here is how Aeriale, the "slow learning disabled" student I quoted earlier, describes the competing voices she hears:

> It took me years to overcome the insecurities and have the courage to go after things I thought I couldn't achieve because of a small weak voice that I still hear telling me "you can't, you aren't able, you have a learning disability, just accept it and settle." Now I live to prove that voice wrong. But you asked why I used *voice* to describe my transformation. It's because I knew what I was capable of. I knew I was smart and talented. But knowing something does no good if you don't act upon it. It wasn't until I started to verbally set my own limits that I started to believe what I knew. It was a power that I gave myself.

As she describes it, this enabling voice is the internalized voices of her own great sidekicks (her Merlins), the great teachers she has benefited from, who convinced her that her difference was not a deficit—and that whatever problems this difference might cause, they can be worked around. That, in Owen's words, she could fulfill her destiny. When she says, "It was a power I gave myself"—we get the doubleness of self: she is both giver and receiver, sidekick and hero of her story.

One of the last images we have of Owen is in a residential home where he was preparing for college and had boldly created a Disney film club that met once a week. As it turned out other students on the autistic spectrum were drawn to Disney, and on the evening Suskind attended they were watching *Dumbo*, a movie about stigma and difference, with the uplifting message—urged on him by his sidekick, a mouse named Timothy—that our differences, like Dumbo's huge ears, could actually be advantages. Suskind stopped the movie to ask those attending if they ever felt they had "special ears," a trait that had made them an outcast but that had also been a real advantage to them. The room got quiet. It was clear that many of these students had rarely, if ever, had their passion for Disney treated as something serious and meaningful.

One young woman talked about how her gentle nature, something that leaves her vulnerable, is a great strength in how she handles rescue dogs. Another mentioned "my brain, because it can take me on adventures of imagination."

After this session, the Disney Club committed to "finding the hidden ears." That, after all, is what Suskind and his family did. They took a trait, easily dismissed as a "problem" for autistic children, Owen's obsessiveness, and turned it into a navigational tool, a rich mythological landscape with companions and guides who could help him with his destiny.

I suspect we will never fully eradicate stigma. One thing societies do is establish norms, and as long as there is normal, there will be abnormal or different, marked as a deficit. That is the story those who need special help often hear, it is what they feel when called out of class for special testing or help, when they struggle to do what their classmates seem to do so easily. As I have talked to those who give and receive this special help, I get the sense that they realize that this "story" cannot be magically eliminated. It is a voice Aeriale still hears.

But with the help of great and committed teachers—those great sidekicks—they can create a different story for themselves. As they become "students of the game," they can tell a more precise story, one in which they are not "dumb" or "behind"—where they can "depersonalize the interior" and be clinical about where they have trouble and how they can work around it. Students can also be affirmed in the fact that intelligence takes many forms, and that our strengths can be mobilized to pull along our weaknesses. We can also tell them the truth—that in the world outside of school you don't have to be good at everything. There is an old Greek saying: "The fox knows many things, but the hedgehog knows one big thing." Hedgehogs often do very well.

In a critical scene in the movie *Apollo 13,* when system after system is failing, when the entire mission seems fated to end in tragedy, the head of Mission Control, Gene Kranz, turns the tide with this question: "Let's look at this thing from a . . . um, from a standpoint of status. What do we got on the spacecraft that's good?"

Not a bad question to ask: "What's good?"

Mindsets for Empathy

In his classic, *Lives on the Boundary* (1989), Mike Rose has a chapter with the arresting title, "I Just Want to Be Average." He is quoting a fellow student in a low track, and the point is this student's lack of motivation, the low ceiling he set for himself. But as I thought about it, we all want to be average. We don't want to stand out, draw attention to ourselves, or if we do draw attention, we want to do so in accepted and approved ways.

To live in a community is to live in a network of norms that we instinctively follow. If we allow someone to enter a busy intersection, we expect a wave acknowledgment, and we are slightly pissed when we don't get it. And on and on. The very word *community* is derived from the Latin word for common, *communis.* When these norms are violated, our reaction—instinctively—is not usually some benevolent appreciation for diversity. It is more likely surprise, annoyance, disapproval. In this sense, stigma is not some aberration, but an ever-present tendency that we deny at our peril.

In one of the edgiest songs in the musical *South Pacific,* a lieutenant describes being taught to be prejudiced—and the refrain is "you have to be carefully taught." It is comforting to imagine that traits like empathy and kindness and inclusiveness and openness are innate and natural—and that the uglier biases and stereotypes come from the outside. But a more realistic view of human nature acknowledges that we all possess a predisposition to divide the world into us and them, to treat differences as deficits, to stigmatize and shun.

Take this situation that I experienced a couple of months ago. I am sitting in the wonderful new library that our town has built. I am reading. And a group of special needs children enters the library, accompanied by two aides who direct them to books and magazines that they might be interested in. The students seem to me "marked" as special needs by a way of walking that I can't pin down, but more obviously by their loudness. The aides reminded them to keep their voices down, but they soon rose to what must have seemed the natural volume to these kids.

A young girl, maybe middle school age, took a seat near me with a pictorial information book on animal facts. After each page, she would exclaim loudly, "Oh boy. Oh boy." I would like to say that my reaction was to be grateful that these kids had the chance to use this library (that my wife and I contributed to). That I was pleased that this book was such a pleasure to this young girl.

But my instinctive reaction was to be annoyed. I'm ashamed to admit this. The calm of the library was disturbed, the norms of speaking violated. I was now distracted. The aides of course knew this, and I waited until one of them urged her gently to speak more quietly, to no avail—and I moved, somewhat grudgingly, to a more remote part of the library where these voices were less audible.

I could multiply this confession with others. When I see a severely physically disabled person, the very rational part of my brain tells me that I should feel empathy for someone like this. But I would be lying to myself if I denied that frisson of bias, even revulsion and avoidance that I feel.

As I thought about this unappealing tendency, I realized that I was locked into what could be called a "fixed mindset" when it came to empathy. It was something you had or didn't have: there were people who were empathetic (naturally) and those who were not (naturally). It was exactly the trap Carol Dweck warns about when it comes to learning. This fixed mindset concerning empathy, I am convinced, can lead to complacency and moral blindness. If we *are* empathetic, it is not something that we have to struggle with; it just flows naturally from our being. If we fail, as I did in the library, it is a basic character flaw.

But what happens if we transpose Dweck's concept of the growth mindset to something like empathy? We can begin by acknowledging that we all possess the capacity to stigmatize; that one thing that human societies do is to create norms, a fantastically complex network of unspoken rules and standards that constitute desired social performances. And like it or not we are bothered by deviations. We may not be able to say exactly how many inches a person should be distant from us when we are talking—but we know when that "rule" is violated. We know when our space is violated. We sense the right decibel level for speaking in a library.

It is liberating to think of empathy not as a fixed trait, one that we have or don't have, but as a struggle, a journey, a perpetual tension—an internal challenge to a deep-seated human tendency toward bias. And there are two tools that we have for this struggle: introspection and familiarity. I can *think through* the situation at the library. First, I can admit to the feeling I had—nothing good comes from lying to ourselves. But I can get over the reflexive annoyance and be happy that this building, that my wife and I helped build, is open to groups like the one that came that day. And, as a better self, I can cherish the girl's unsubdued delight in what she was reading.

The other tool is familiarity. I recently attended the final reading at the Writers Academy that I helped establish about twenty years ago. One reader on the final day was a young girl with severe multiple sclerosis that affected her voice so that she read in a bare whisper, almost inaudible. When it came her turn to read, a classmate helped her to the front of the room and stood beside her in support (she and others also helped this girl get from class to class). These were not longtime friends—they had just gotten to know her during the week of the academy. This girl confidently read her story, and received her applause. We couldn't really hear the words, but appreciated the fact that she was reading. Whatever discomfort we felt, or she felt, seemed to melt into the celebration of her writing.

II

ASKING AND RECEIVING

(CHAPTER 4)

"To the one who knocks, the door will be opened."

To ask without shame.

—**AMANDA PALMER,** *THE ART OF ASKING*

For my entire college teaching career, I was required to have office hours, two or three a week. The theory behind office hours was fine—to make faculty regularly available to students who might need help on assignments or papers. They could make appointments or just drop in unannounced, and I would be there.

It just never worked that way. Now, I consider myself a fairly congenial, open, "laid-back" (as my students write on evaluations) teacher, but students didn't drop in or even call for appointments during this time. They didn't use office hours, and I would regularly take this time to catch up on email or recommendation letters. It was not that most students couldn't use this opportunity—to talk through their plans for a paper, for example. But students would very rarely come in and say something like, "Here's my plan for the profile paper. I'd like to get your reaction to it."

There are several possible explanations for this failure to take advantage of office hours:

- Students work so close to the deadline that the timing is off to get early help.
- Seeking help in this way makes the student appear too invested in school work. It feels like grade grubbing, even bordering on cheating. You need to keep your distance.
- If suggestions for improvements are offered, this will create an expectation or obligation for the student. That is, the teacher may look to see if advice has been taken—and be disappointed if it is not.
- Seeking help is perceived as an admission of inadequacy or failure, which would be better to hide. Students want to think of themselves as good students, competent students, and asking for help would undermine that identity. So they vote with their feet—better to risk a poor grade than seek help.
- To the extent that students did come, it was often the better-prepared, more confident students who took advantage—so a practice that was meant to level the playing field only tilted it more.
- No matter how open the professor's door, there is often the perception of interruption or intrusion—the student is disrupting important work.
- The issue of social class may also play into this reluctance. A professor is seen as a member of an elite group—I'm Dr. Newkirk. And students may feel intimidated by what they perceive as a cultural divide.
- Students don't know *how* to seek help. Though faculty might view help seeking as a self-evident skill, it clearly is not. It requires the capacity to define a problem that you want help on—and often the student has only a global feeling of confusion. In effect, seeking help can compound the embarrassment of the student. (1) It can be embarrassing to seek help in the first place, and (2) it can be embarrassing to have difficulty describing the help you want.

Just making this list made me more aware of the complexity of help seeking, and the reasons why students might feel hesitant or resistant.

In any potential help-seeking situation, there also is a question of threshold—at what point is help seeking appropriate. Set the threshold too low, for something truly minor, and we can feel we are wasting the professional's time. But—and here is the true danger—set it too high and a minor problem can mutate into a far less manageable one. Christine Harris, a psychology professor specializing in social emotions including embarrassment, has documented that women in particular may be prone to avoiding medical help "to avoid looking silly or feeling embarrassed if the symptom turned out to have a trivial cause" (2006, 533). She concludes that "delaying or not seeking medical attention because of embarrassment threat may be a substantial cause of avoidable mortality or morbidity" (533).

Take this example: when my parents were in their eighties, my father developed what turned out to be colon cancer and could not make it to the bathroom. So he arranged to sit on a chair on a throw rug that my mother, frail and in her eighties as well, would grip and use to drag him to the bathroom. It was weeks before my physician brother and I learned of this procedure (that they both claimed "worked fine"). Of course, it is easy to fall into a dangerous cycle: set the threshold high and the situation gets worse, which means that seeking help becomes harder—the embarrassment of seeking help is compounded by the embarrassment of waiting.

This resistance to care was so strongly rooted in my father, and passed on to me, that I decided to interview a local primary care physician in my town, known for his deep solicitude for patients. On a sunny spring Saturday, with daffodils up and the local forsythia bushes brilliant yellow, I sat down with Kenny Rotner to probe this resistance.

He sees the resistance to help seeking as grounded in a basic (and irrational) capacity for denial:

> Very strongly wired into human nature is denial—the ability to block things out. And as irrational as it is, people feel that if I don't pay attention to something, it's not going to be a problem. If you take screening for colon cancer—there's a good percentage of people who don't have colonoscopies, and in their mind they develop the scheme that if I don't have a colonoscopy I won't have colon cancer.

It's as if the test creates (rather than detects) the problem.

Stigma, shame, embarrassment are also big barriers.

> I'm struck by how often people have problems they feel are very different from everyone else's. I hear from people that they're having an issue and they feel unique, singled out in having an issue, alone in it. And when

> people have a problem they feel guilty about it. Something's wrong. They didn't do something right—it's a negative judgment on them. So people avoid care because they feel they are very unique, alone and isolated.

We are addicted to a type of self-narrative in which we are heroes. "I am the master of my fate/I am the captain of my soul." So when the soul is troubled it must be bad steering by the captain—particularly in the cases of psychological distress.

> People feel embarrassed to come to a doctor. Let's say that their quality of life is affected by depression. People feel that they should be able, on their own, to say that "I'm not going to be depressed. I'm going to be OK." So that people will somaticize it—so they say that they're tired. But as the relationship develops, and they feel that they're accepted—people become more forthcoming and more honest.

Part of that acceptance is "letting them know that they are not alone."

Vulnerability and Avoidance

In the case of many of my students, the results of not seeking help are not life altering—but for some students they can be. In an incredibly touching episode of *This American Life*, we meet Jonathan Gonzalez. Jonathan went to a tough high school in the Bronx, but earned a scholarship to Wheaton College where he slowly sank from view and, like many students in his situation, failed to graduate. He was part of the 80 percent of students in the lowest income brackets that don't make it, a national tragedy (Korn 2015). But it wasn't purely or even primarily a lack of preparation that did him in; it was a sense of embarrassment, a feeling that he stood out, did not belong.

In his first days at Wheaton, he panicked when he looked at the syllabus—all those books that he couldn't afford. He didn't tell anyone he couldn't afford them, and just went on without them.

> I didn't do the homework, so I'm going now into a class where, one, it's a different dynamic. Now I'm in Fieldston [an affluent private school he visited in high school], where it's twelve kids to a teacher, and I'm the only black kid in some of these classes. I'm the only kid in some of these classes.

> So now I'm embarrassed to be the only black guy that doesn't do the work and fulfill that stereotype. So I'm not going to class. It's a catch-22, because now I'm still the black kid now that just doesn't come to class, and doesn't do the work on top of that. But for me, it was—I mean, what am I going to say to these teachers?
>
> I need to go to class. You need to talk to somebody. And then there's another voice that's like, no, you're going to be embarrassed. It's embarrassing. Anyway, you're not going to have the money, so how is that going to help?
>
> Asking for help is being vulnerable. And the only person I was vulnerable with was Raquel [his girlfriend]. And sometimes I would just lie, like, yeah, I did homework today. (Joffe-Walt 2015)

With some help, Raquel learned that they could get the books they needed from the library, and she told Jonathan this news, but he was too far gone to take this help.

I am sure that schools like Wheaton have writing centers, and academic counselors, even bridge programs for students like Jonathan and Raquel. But there is a double bind that operates here. And Jonathan touches on it in his interview. If he reaches out for help, if for example he asks his advisor if he can get help buying his books (possibly part of his scholarship), he makes himself "vulnerable"; he is confirming the stereotype that he doesn't belong, that he doesn't even have the means to buy the books. If he goes for tutoring, he confirms the stereotype that he doesn't really belong, that he's not ready. It's what social psychologist Claude Steele (2011) calls a "stereotype threat."

And if he fails to get help, and does poorly, he *also* confirms the stereotype. It's a catch-22, exactly. Is it any wonder that the way out of this situation is to find a way to be kicked out of school? Better not to try.

Seeking help is hardly a rational process of self-improvement. Seeking help, for example, aligns the learner with the institution of school—it announces that doing well matters to the student. It is not difficult though to imagine how public displays of caring, of wanting to do well, can be threatening.

We see it all the time in schools, for example, students bragging about *how little* they studied for a test. In a conversation with University of New Hampshire Writing Center Director Molly Tetreault, I was surprised to learn that even in our college, this threat is very present and can create awkwardness in tutoring sessions. To begin with, males come through the writing center doors far less frequently than females (a national trend) even though the evidence is clear they have more writing difficulties. So even to *be there* can mark the student as being too eager, too nerdy. One protective strategy, then, is to distance oneself from the task: it's just a paper, just a hoop I have to jump through. It's not really about me. I suspect students assume this posture even if secretly doing well, becoming a more successful writer, does matter to them.

I saw this firsthand when I began my first teaching position (1970) in a largely African American public school in the Roxbury section of Boston. Many of the students there were biding their time until they could leave at sixteen; although most didn't want that, they still had to take the pose that school (or at least English taught by a white twenty-three-year-old man) didn't matter to them.

In a grand piece of school theatre, one of my tenth graders, Butch Whittaker, taught me that lesson. Butch had failed the first term, and another term like that could cause him to be held back. So Butch began to goof off less and work more—and on one spelling test he got a perfect 100 and an A. I still picture Butch: athletic, a huge Afro haircut where he sometimes stored his pencil, still a slight drawl from the South where he was born. Butch picked up his test paper, walked slowly, slowly to the trash can, folded it, tore it in halves, quarters, eighths, and then bits that fluttered down into the can. He turned to his classmates, "This is what I do with my As."

It was a perfect, perfect performance—letting his classmates know he got an A, and showing (or pretending to show) it didn't matter. He could thread the needle between caring and not caring.

There is no question that this code is a barrier. Boys who must take on a posture of indifference to protect their male identities carry a heavy handicap. Clarence Page, an African American columnist for the *Chicago Tribune*, once observed how this oppositional attitude ("If you try or care you are being 'white'") can take hold. Peers police peers. "With friends like that," he lamented, "who needs enemies?"

Even in the wider culture, boys often believe that they can make an end run around the educational system—that the qualities developed on the sports fields and friendship groups (assertiveness, bravery, humor) will matter most in the end. Bart Simpson believes that if he ever grows up he will be Lisa's boss—despite her hugely superior academic record.

In *Lives on the Boundary* (1989), Mike Rose probes this identity of not caring. The trigger for his analysis was a comment from a vocationally tracked student, who when challenged by his teacher responded, "I just want to be average." Why, Rose puzzled, would a student *want* to be average? His answer is that to try, to care, is to invite frustration and possible failure. Better to reject is all: "Champion the average. Rely on your own good common sense. Fuck this bullshit."

But the cost of this defense is devastating. Rose writes:

> The tragedy is that you have to twist the knife in your own gray matter to make the defense work. You'll have to shut down, have to reject intellectual stimuli or defuse them with sarcasm, have to cultivate stupidity, have to convert boredom from a malady into a way of confronting the world. Keep your vocabulary simple, act stoned when you're not or act more stoned than you are, flaunt ignorance. . . . It is a powerful and effective defense. . . . But like all strong magic, it exacts a price. (1989, 28)

Even in the earlier grades we can see the teaching challenge exponentially increase as *a difficulty becomes an identity* ("I hate reading. Books are stupid, boring.").

I recall vividly another incident from my years teaching in Boston. Some new books had arrived and the head of our department, Frank Sullivan, was showing them to a student.

"I've already seen these," the student said. My colleague explained that these were newly published books and there is no way he could have seen them.

"Man, I'm telling you I've *seen* these books before."

Frank came back, "Son [yes he did use that word], you couldn't have seen them. They're new."

And at this point the student did something I'll never forget. He grabbed one of the books, began turning pages.

"Look man, words, just words. I've seen these books."

Books were just an interchangeable source of irritation.

And yet I also believe that in an age that produces more reading and demands more writing than at any other point in history—no one truly wants to be a poor reader or writer. We need to look beyond the posture of indifference, or just see it as a posture. One thing our good teachers (and parents) did was to take us seriously, to imagine, for example, that our writing could truly reflect and convey our thinking, that it could say things we wanted to say. That it could be done. That books (or the right book) could speak to us, that there were authors out there who were writing for us. If we are taken seriously by others, we have a fighting chance to learn to take ourselves seriously, to invest and care.

Coaching

Embarrassment, or the fear of it, also limits us as teachers. Dramatically. It keeps us isolated, silent, and reluctant to seek help.

There was one point in my career when I truly needed help. It was a busy time for me—demands of my family, aging parents, publishing expectations, major administrative duties, frequent speaking engagements. Up to this point I had been doing well, even winning a university teaching award. But my teaching was on a decline. Semester after semester my writing classes seemed flat; they didn't become the communities I heard my fellow teachers describe, and I often didn't look forward to teaching them, though I denied that feeling. I was slow to learn names, or put them in my grade books, signs I refused to register. To be sure, these classes were not disasters, but not what they should have been. As Dante says in the opening to *The Inferno*: "Midway upon the journey of our life I found myself within a forest dark, for the straightforward pathway had been *lost*." And he adds, "Ah me! How hard a thing it is to say" (Longfellow 2010).

This went on too long, until I received a negative five-year review and a stern letter from the dean that jolted me into a change. It was humiliating at the time, and in my defensiveness I thought it unfair. But eventually I came to admit that I needed to be more *present* in the classroom, as a model, storyteller—I needed to make more of an effort to get to know each student individually. I improved, and did my best teaching after that, but a true regret of my career is that it took so long. I regret I failed to take assistance from my colleagues—who surely would have helped me out.

I realize that there can be logistical difficulties in peer review—freeing time for peer coaches, training them to be effective, finding time for debriefing, keeping these exchanges entirely separate from any formal evaluation. But if schools can manage a bus schedule, they can surely manage this. I am convinced these obstacles could be surmounted if we as teachers overcame our fear of embarrassment, of being exposed. Atul Gawande, surgeon and writer for *The New Yorker*, identifies the issue:

> It will never be easy to submit to coaching, especially for those who are well along in their career. I'm ostensibly an expert. I'd finished long ago with the days of being tested and observed. I am supposed to be past needing such things. Why should I expose myself to scrutiny and fault-finding? (2011)

Using himself as a case study, Gawande shows that even an accomplished surgeon in midcareer can make improvements. Thinking that his performance level had plateaued (at a high level to be sure), he bravely invites a former teacher to watch him, and for the first time in eight years he gets advice that helps him improve. Some of it involved small adjustments—adjusting the lighting so that his assistants can see more clearly. Some was more significant, thinking through how to maintain tension on a tumor so that it can be more cleanly removed.

I could have done the same thing. I had peers that could have come in and offered advice. What kept me back, what prevented me even from considering this option, was embarrassment, the fear of exposure, of having someone see that I had difficulty. Ego. Pride. After all, I taught the practicum course for new teachers in the program. I wrote articles on teaching writing. I was supposed to be an expert. In sweet retrospect, I now realize that I would have been a better model for them if I had asked for help—and shared that process with them.

In her book, *The Gifts of Imperfection* (2010), Brené Brown makes an observation about seeking help that caught me up short, that seemed directed at me. She notes that many of us construct our lives in an imbalanced way, particularly as teachers. We are happy, gratified to offer help—that is a big part of our professional identity. But we (or at least I) are far more reluctant to *receive* help. Brown makes the claim that "until we receive with an open heart, we are never really giving with an open heart" (2010, 20). It's another version of an argument I have made all my professional life—that to teach writing, you have to be a writer. Otherwise, there are awarenesses, what D. H. Lawrence called "blood consciousness," that we never gain. Physicians, for example, typically attest to the fact that they learn a great deal when they are patients.

We can also forget that openly seeking help can itself be an act of generosity. We can easily fall into the trap of seeing help seeking as a game of subtraction—there is the giver and the receiver. The receiver subtracts from the giver. We are taking something. We imagine the giver as generous, but fail to see the generosity in our very request. We fail to imagine that the help seeker is also a giver. The offer of vulnerability and trust is precious, something we as teachers treasure—it helps make possible a relationship where both giver and receiver benefit. It's a big part of the reason we all wanted to become teachers in the first place.

This is not mere sentimentality, a pleasurable fuzzy feeling of being helpful. Even more hard-edged professionals in business management stress the point that getting help is not a zero sum game—that in fact the giver, the teacher, is an equal or even greater beneficiary. Adam Grant cites research explaining one of the major reasons firstborn siblings tend to outperform their younger brothers and sisters: they take on the role of teacher and that "the teacher gains more than the learner in the process of teaching" (2016, SR 3).

As an example, a friend of mine, who has two boys, one in kindergarten and one in middle school, was discussing with her husband the possibility of a third child. The older boy, overhearing the conversation, sighed and said, "Guys, I don't think I can do this again!"

Grant also stresses that even in that seemingly most individualistic modern profession—investment banking—analysts cannot rely on raw brainpower. Rather, they work in institutions with "distributed intelligence"—that is, the institution knows more than any one person possibly can. Success comes from collaborative teamwork where the analyst can seek out information and gain skills from others (the same could be said for writing a book like this one).

I also think of my wife's relationship to her physician, the wonderful care Dr. Pettinari has given as she dealt with diabetes and endometrial cancer, along with the nagging condition of growing older. My wife and I both have profound gratitude for this level of care. It is harder to see, though, that my wife is offering something back, an openness about her health, a trust in the decisions that Dr. Pettinari makes, fidelity to the course of treatment prescribed, along with the candor to say when something doesn't seem to be working. It is easy, I feel, to miss this reciprocity.

The possibility of embarrassment is compounded, I think, by unrealistic images of success or excellence. One feature of Goffman's concept of performance is "idealization": we carry with us models of the role we are performing—parent, husband, teacher. To quote Robert Park again: "So far as the mask represents the conception we have formed of ourselves—the role we are striving to live up to—this mask is the truer self, the self we would like to be" (Goffman 1963). This is as it should be—we don't need to invent the world; we live in societies that provide us models and goals to strive for. Our reach must exceed our grasp and all that.

But there is danger here as well—the lurking feeling that no matter how hard we try, we don't measure up. Just as young girls compare themselves unfavorably to models, teachers can imagine themselves in competition with superteachers—the pedagogical equivalent to Beyoncé. Idealization gone amok. So long as we stay within our classrooms, we can imagine how far short of this ideal we fall. But if we could break free of this isolation, we could explode this image, and get a truer, more realistic picture of excellence.

Help Seeking as Performance

> *In order for help seeking to be both effective and instrumental, the individual must know enough to know what is not known, to know what could be known, and to have some reasonable ideas about where and how such knowledge might be gained.*
>
> —SHARON NELSON-LE GALL, "HELP-SEEKING BEHAVIOR IN LEARNING"

Asking for help is a performance, one that can be invisible to those for whom it is now "natural." Linguist and literacy specialist James Gee relates this uncomfortable story:

> A foreign doctoral student in graduate school in the United States has, after several years in her program, lost her PhD advisor. She needs to get another one. She is talking to a professor who she wants as an advisor, but who is reluctant to take her on as a student. Facing this reluctance, she says: "It's your job to help me, I need to learn." (2014)

I think we instantly recognized that in this situation, the student needed to frame a real *request*, even a persuasive appeal. Her neediness is not enough (or the right) kind of appeal. She needed to frame her request something like, "My advisor will be on leave next year and can't work with me. I was wondering of you could take her place. I think my project fits well with your own research. . . ." In reality, there are cases where, as a professor in a small specialty area, you do *have to* take on a stranded student, but there is a protocol for asking.

On the other side of the coin, there are students who are paralyzed to ask for letters of recommendation and imagine it as an imposition on me and my colleagues, when in fact, we see it as part of our professional duties. Again there is a protocol for asking, usually offering to provide a curriculum vitae and even copies of previous papers, but because these letters are required for the next step in their careers, they are clearly entitled to have us write them. It is one form of privilege or entitlement to be able to perform these requests properly, to frame a request, but to also expect those in authority to work as your ally.

Part of the performance of help seeking involves the capacity to describe a problem. In his classic book, *How We Think* (1910), John Dewey views the act of thought as beginning in a global feeling of unease—something is awry, a trusted routine seems not to be working, we have a gut feeling that we have made a wrong step, a wrong decision. It is primarily an emotional sense, still undefined or not described. According to Dewey a key, perhaps *the* key, act of thought is translation—to move from a felt sense of a problem to something more analytical: a possible cause, something that can be conveyed to a doctor, or therapist, or teacher.

The Locked Door

Imagine, if you will, a Mexican American mother, who at times struggles with her English, at the door of her son's school. Like most schools these days it is locked. She pulls the door a couple of times. Then she looks around and sees cameras mounted above the doors so she assumes that she is being watched by someone. She waits for someone to open the door.

She finally finds a small console beside the door, with a button, and what she thinks is a section for speaking into it. Tentatively she presses the button, and she hears a disembodied voice that asks, "How can I help you?"

She is flustered, flushed, and feels her English abandon her. After a couple false starts, she blurts out, "I'm here about Ramon."

The voice responds, "And which teacher do you want to see?"

She couldn't remember the name, it was an unfamiliar English name—and she had it written down on an envelope in her purse. She fumbles to try to find it, too many pockets in that purse. It is here somewhere. Somewhere.

After a long pause, and much fumbling, the voice relents: "Come on in." She hears a soft buzz and the door opens. Unnerved, she walks toward the main office.

One of my favorite PBS shows is *Car Talk,* featuring Tom and Ray Magliozzi who introduce themselves this way: "Ever wonder just exactly what kind of nature, nurture, and arrested socialization led to the development of two demented troglodytes like us? Sociologists at major universities have been asking the same question for years!" The great feature of the show is how motorists with car problems explain their problems—they tell about the origins of the problem, create sound effects to simulate what they experience, and detail remedies suggested by friends ("This week on *The Best of Car Talk,* Jill's pal keeps telling her she needs to do more highway driving to 'blow the stuff' out of her car. Jill's not opposed to this, but what exactly is she trying to blow out?"). Tom and Ray, of course, only play dumb—what we have is an expert help-seeking situation, and I'm sure contestants are chosen because they can vividly portray their car troubles.

On the other side of the coin, we tend to avoid situations where we cannot perform this role of help seeker, where we imagine we will only feel stupider than we already feel—which is invariably my case when asking for computer help. The conversation usually goes something like this:

Computer Geek: OK what browser do you use?

Me: Comcast.

CG: Comcast is not a browser. It's your cable provider.

Me: Microsoft Office?

CG: That's a set of programs. I'm thinking of something like Internet Explorer.

Me: Oh yeah, that's what I use.

CG: Which version, 8, 9, 10, 11?

Me: I don't know—it's just that *E* thing with the ring around it.

And so on. I feel like an idiot already. I feel sorry for the poor technician, usually some guy in his twenties, who has to walk me though this terminology.

I know I am not alone in this perpetually embarrassing situation—Bill Bryson tells his own version of this story and concludes: "This you see, is why I don't call the computer helpline very often. We've been talking four seconds and already I can feel the riptide of ignorance and shame pulling me into the icy depths of Humiliation Bay" (1999, 28). I know that I avoid encounters like this as much as I can, because they make me feel inadequate and stupid because I cannot perform the help-seeking role effectively. Imagine how much more difficult it is for those who begin with the burden of a bias against them: the classic case of a woman getting help with a car. How any indecision or confusion works to confirm a stereotype.

But if there is a positive lesson to pull from these painful encounters, it is this: to seek help, it is useful to possess a minimal working vocabulary, knowing for example the difference between an operating system, a server, and a search engine. In the case of writing, the minimal vocabulary might look something like this:

- language to describe the writing process—*prewriting, drafting, revision editing, brainstorming, freewriting, webbing*
- language to describe the basic qualities of writing—*focus, voice, order, pace, clutter*
- language to describe features of writing—*lead, detail, evidence, conclusion, point, counterargument, plot*
- language to name the kind of writing being attempted—*commentary, letter to the editor, lab report, memoir, profile.*

Across the country students are sent to writing centers to get this help—it's all about sentences and errors. Even faculty, often brilliant in their field, can lack a vocabulary to describe the help students need, particularly the bigger cognitive work that needs to be done.

Even this handful of terms would enable students to *name* the problem or issue they are dealing with, to move beyond a global sense that they are stuck. Otherwise students can feel doubly incompetent: they have trouble with their writing, and trouble saying what that trouble is.

When students lack this language, they revert to a cultural commonplace about writing problems—they say they "need help with their grammar." This is not surprising because we all know the widespread complaint that students can't write sentences these days (not at all true in my opinion). Across the country students are sent to writing centers to get this help—it's all about sentences and errors. Even faculty, often brilliant in their field, can lack a vocabulary to describe the help students need, particularly the bigger cognitive work that needs to be done.

In addition to knowing this terminology, another tip would be to make an attempt at the problem, assignment, paper before the meeting. If it is a written assignment, come in with a plan for the paper, a strategy, the opening page of a draft, something. It's similar to guiding a bicycle—it's easier if the rider is in motion rather than at a standstill. A teacher has a better chance of helping a student who has at least tried to formulate a plan than one who says, "I don't know where to begin. I'm lost."

The protocol, the etiquette, of seeking help is anything but self-evident. I will give you one more common misstep. A student asks to see me because he "really wants an A in the course." This is perfectly reasonable and perhaps the real motivation for seeking help. But for most teachers I know, it is a bad first move. It suggests that the student's real motivation is the reward of a grade and not learning the skill or content being taught; the student using this as an opening fails to present himself or herself as a *learner*. And the student fails to recognize that I don't see myself as primarily a grade dispenser.

Researchers in help seeking make a crucial distinction between executive and instrumental help (Nelson-Le Gall 1985). Executive help is dependency-oriented and aimed at "fixing" a particular problem. We participate in this form of help seeking all the time, for example, when we get the pilot light on our furnace fixed. We may be mildly curious about what caused our problem, but we depend on the mechanic to do the work. A mismatch occurs when a student takes this "fixing" orientation into a learning situation. This is probably the case with the example about getting an A—"Just tell me what I need to do."

In instrumental situations the student needs to be a more active participant—not turning over responsibility to the tutor or teacher. There is an expectation or some self-diagnosis on the part of the student, some sense of where in the process he or she is finding difficulty. As Nelson-Le Gall puts it: "If individuals have some awareness of the complexity of the task and can monitor their progress on the task well enough to detect a problem, they are in a relatively good position to utilize help seeking as a strategy" (1985, 71). Furthermore, the point of the consultation is to cooperatively model a *process* that has utility beyond the specific task, one that can at some point be internalized. One mantra in writing centers is to "teach the writer and not the writing."

When a student with this "fixing" orientation comes to office hours or a tutoring session—there is what Goffman calls a failure, at least initially, to establish a common "situation definition," and the potential for frustration and embarrassment. Students can feel that they are not getting real help ("Why all these questions?"), and the instructor can feel frustrated at the dependency the student is seeking. Unless the student can learn to become a reciprocal partner, the consultation will work at cross-purposes.

Another possibility is that the teacher will become a fixer. The situation definition will shift to one of executive help and dependency. It's so easy to do under time pressure or sympathy for the learner. This shift is particularly seductive for special education aides who may keenly feel the frustration of the children they work with. I remember one case, in particular, where an aide, working with a first-grade boy who had difficulty spelling, became a scribe for all of his writing. He created vivid and detailed stories, but made little progress that I could see in becoming an independent writer.

Coaching

But how on earth can these tacit, usually unspoken rules of help seeking be learned?

Some students surely pick up these conventions osmotically—one form privilege takes is contact with a network of supporting adults. Children who come from the upper socioeconomic strata often have a huge advantage here because they typically have extensive experience conversing with adults, often professionals, as conversational equals. From a very early age they are expected to have—and express—preferences, opinions, and they even have the entitlement to disagree. It is common for them to address seeming authority figures on a first-name basis. Consequently, their upbringing prepares them to be relatively unintimidated by a professional hierarchy, or not experience it as a hierarchy at all.

They know the convention of asking for help. Others may need coaching.

Paradoxically, one form of privilege is the belief that you are entitled to help—that the resources of a school are there for you. Anthony Abraham Jack, now a doctoral student at Harvard, tells this story:

> I grew up supported by a security guard's wages in a predominantly black Miami neighborhood in a single-parent household. For senior year I switched from a public high school to a private one after growing tired of being treated as an athlete-student instead of the other way around. My new school, Gulliver Preparatory School, showed me how

> the other 1 percent lived. But I learned much more even in that one year. I discovered that visiting faculty in their offices to talk things through wasn't an imposition, but an expectation. I learned that I didn't just need to make demands on myself, but I could make demands on others. (2015, 12)

In institutions like the ones I have taught in, writing centers and other sources of academic assistance (including office hours) are underutilized—particularly early in a semester or term, and particularly by freshmen, many of whom can coast through this first year.

> Paradoxically, one form of privilege is the belief that you are entitled to help—that the resources of a school are there for you.

Jeff Nelson, CEO of OneGoal, has committed himself to helping disadvantaged college students from Chicago to use that first year as a "magical time frame" to catch up. Students in the OneGoal Program are coached on how to seek assistance. For example, Kewauna, in a challenging lecture course at Western Illinois:

> On the first day of class, Kewauna did what Michele Stefl [a teacher in OneGoal] had recommended: she politely introduced herself to the professor and then took a seat in the front row, which, until Kewauna sat down was occupied entirely by white girls, which disappointed Kewauna. The other African-American students all tended to sit in the back, which disappointed Kewauna ("That's what they *expect* you to do . . . . Back in the civil rights movement, if they told you to sit in the back, you wouldn't do it."). (Tough 2012, 173)

When she took notes she starred words she was unfamiliar with and, at the end of the lecture she went through them, one by one, with the lecturer. She attended office hours with all her professors, made friends with other students in the classes who could sometimes help her with assignments, and used the writing center. Like Anthony Jack, she learned how "to make demands on others" and not go it alone. She used resources that were freely available.

Jack concludes that "being at ease with individuals in positions of authority, especially those who act as gatekeepers to resources" is as valuable a life skill as the more academic skills and knowledge gained in school.

My oldest daughter, somehow, gained this ease early in her life—in fact I can't remember when she didn't have it. She didn't get it from me. One time, when she was about twelve, we were at a reception at Colby College where my future sister-in-law taught piano. Sarah happened to be standing beside a tall, dignified older man, and she asked him what he did.

"I'm actually the Provost here at Colby."

"Oh," she responded. "The Big Cheese."

He smiled and said, "Yes, the Big Cheese."

* * * *

To return to the failure of office hours. The practice seems built on a belief in the rationality of students: if a person needs help, he or she will seek it out. It is prudent self-interest to take advantage of resources that will help us achieve our goals. You build it and they will come. This kind of rationale has long been a staple in orthodox economic theory—get the incentives right and you can predict behavior. But recently an entire field of behavioral economics has evolved that explores the irrationality—the biases that work against self-interest—we are all prone to. Scholars like Daniel Kahneman, Amos Tversky, and Richard Thaler have explored the systematic biases that shape economic decision-making, often to our disadvantage. I have already alluded to one tendency—loss aversion—that causes us to *feel* losses more acutely than gains, a bias that often prevents us from taking "good" risks.

One example of behavioral bias is the failure of employees to contribute to health plans even when there is a decent match from employers. This bias is called "present bias": discounting rewards that are distant in time. These employees "know" that saving early is important, that people don't save enough, that social security won't be adequate (or even there) when they retire . . . but the "default" (the standard setting) is not signing up. It takes a positive action to opt in.

Cass Sunstein and Richard Thaler (2009) argue that behavior can be changed with "nudges" that change the default—still allowing employees to choose not to contribute, *but they have to make a choice not to contribute*. The default is set at participating in plans. While clearly controversial (some say it makes for a kind of paternalism), Sunstein and Thaler claim that changing the default can help employees make better choices without infringing on personal freedom.

One way to change the help-seeking default in schools is to make it expected. We apply this principle in health care when we schedule annual physicals or semiannual visits to the dentist. We make it *normal*. I have much different luck if I schedule regular conferences with students—this practice suggests that getting help is not something you do in a time of crisis, or when you have a "problem." It is normal, an expected part of the writing process. For years, I would have biweekly conferences with students—some came under duress, to be sure, but for many it was the first (and sadly only) time they had one-on-one conversations with faculty. At recommendation time, they came to their writing teachers for recommendations, even when their major was on the other side of campus.

This normalization of difficulty is a central theme of Peter Johnston's (2004) work. He encourages teachers to use prompts like, "Who came up with an interesting problem?" Looking for trouble may not always be a good posture to take in life, but it is the mark of a good thinker. Failure or disappointment is less scary if we can name it, share it, and see it as a normal and expected feature of thinking and working. Or as Brené Brown writes: shame "hates having words wrapped around it —it can't survive being shared" (2010, 10).

Falling

Climbing Mount Katahdin is one of the great thrills, and challenges, in New England. One route up takes you across the "Knife Edge," a very narrow, totally exposed ridge with almost vertical walls on either side. One recent summer, I hiked it with two of my friends. Early in the hike I raked my shin over a rock—this would normally create nothing more than a scrape, but the notoriously grainy Katahdin rock sliced my shin, and it began to bleed steadily. My friends managed to tape gauze over it, but I was slowly dripping blood.

We managed the heart-stopping section of the Knife Edge, but on my way to the summit I lost my balance. It is absolutely critical to keep your momentum forward and not step backward (where you cannot see where you are stepping). I tumbled backward, bracing my fall with my left hand. Stunned, I waited for my friends who saw that my right palm was now a bloody mess, and my forearm was badly scraped. More gauze and tape. I had one more minor fall before the summit, so now both arms were scraped. I was rattled—and we still had five hours of difficult hiking to get back to our campsite.

I slowly regained my composure, and in a couple of hours we were halfway down at Chimney Pond. As we entered the campsite there, a young woman, younger than my own daughters, came up to me and said, "I think you should have those cuts looked at." I brushed her off, "Thanks but I'm OK."

We walked a bit farther. "Look," she said, "those cuts look bad. I saw them on the top. I'm an emergency room doc and I'd like to look at them." Still reluctant (can doctors look that young?), I followed her to a rock by the pond, and she took out her prodigious first-aid kit and began to take off the badly unraveling gauze and tape. Using a small forceps, she picked out gravel from each cut, applied antiseptic ("This is going to hurt, but you don't want those to get infected"), and reapplied new bandages. When she finished one cut, she'd ask, "Is there another?" and we worked our way from the gash on the shin to the cuts on my hand and both forearms.

It's hard to describe but I melted into that care. It felt so reassuring to watch her work on the cuts, feeling her touch, listening to her narration of what she was doing. It was such a relief to no longer be tough and stoic. By the time she was done, I felt whole and confident. I tried to offer some way of making some kind of donation to charity as a way of thanks, but she waved me off.

As our group started back down to camp, she asked, "By the way, do you take baby aspirin every day?" I admitted I didn't.

"You really should."

(CHAPTER 5)

Soft Hands

He had one of those rare smiles with a quality of eternal reassurance in it that you may come across four or five times in life. It faced, or seemed to face, the whole external world for an instant and then concentrated on you with an irresistible prejudice in your favor. It understood you just as far as you wanted to be understood, believed in you as you would like to believe in yourself.

—**F. SCOTT FITZGERALD,** *THE GREAT GATSBY*

"Soft hands" is not a slogan for some overpriced lotion. It's a football term, applied to pass receivers who seem to cradle the ball, absorbing the speed of the throw. Passes seem to settle into their hands, and not deflect away. It's a term I have used to describe great teaching, specifically the way great teachers make student contributions seem special and smart. It's an elusive quality, like Gatsby's smile, which I will explore in this chapter.

I'll begin with a story told by Ian Fleischer, a fifth-grade teacher who seems to me a parable of great instruction and an illustration of soft hands:

> It was the end of the year and we were doing a journalism study as the last writing unit. We were doing a newspaper, and I thought it would be good to go to the *Portsmouth Herald* and see how newspapers are made. We could bike there. It's not too far, and I had mapped out a route that was safe. So I told my class of fifth graders, "Let's go on this bike trip."
>
> They were very excited. Except Amy. Amy was a shy self-conscious girl, not on any athletic teams, quiet. I realized that there was some problem here, and

I needed to touch base with her. So I took her aside and asked her if she was concerned about the trip. She was evasive: "I don't think I can make it." "My bike is broken." "I don't have a bike I can use." "I don't like to ride a bike." "I don't think I can ride that far." I said, "I can help you with that. I can get you a bike, and we can train together." She agreed, a big risk for her.

I arranged to work with her in an area behind the school where students wouldn't see her—every day at 11:30 the kids had a special, art or music or gym—and Amy and I would go out back, and nobody would be there for forty minutes. We worked for two weeks with nobody around. I brought in my son Owen's bike to school for her. But when I saw her get on the bike, how awkward and tentative she was, I realized that she had probably never been on a bike before. It was very foreign to her. Eleven years old and couldn't ride a bike.

I realized this was not the bike to start her on. I said that was enough for now, and I brought in a smaller bike the next day so she would sit on the seat with her feet on the ground and walk, not even worry about pedaling. So first she would move on the pavement, moving her feet, getting the feel of the handlebars, sitting on the seat. It wasn't more than two days after that she would walk the bike to the grass, and there was a small hill and she would pick up her feet and coast down the hill, over and over again. The next step: "Try to coast with your feet on the pedals." And she would do that. And the next step was: "Put your feet on the pedals and brake." This bike had foot brakes. So she got used to putting her feet on the pedals and stopping. And I thought that was huge because she knew she could stop the bike.

The next step was "pedal forward" as the hill straightened out. "Don't stop. Keep pedaling." And we made a chart, and I put it in the closet, so other kids couldn't see it. But we charted how many pedals she did a day. Five pedals to twenty to fifty to 150. We made a bar chart that we would color in together. And that's how it went for the entire first week. By the end she was pedaling 150 pedals across the field.

She wasn't frustrated. There was one rainy day, and I said, "Amy, we don't have to go out today." But she said, "I want to go out." I put on my raincoat and we were out in the rain doing this. There definitely was something overriding the embarrassment of not knowing how to ride a bike at eleven years old.

By the end of the first week I definitely didn't need to coax her at all. So then the second week we were doing a little more riding on the pavement, doing what we had done on the grass, learning how to fall—what do you do when you fall. More riding back and forth doing turns. And then we started going up and down the street behind the school, farther and farther (we were still keeping track of the pedals). We kept graphing it—but at some point we stopped because it was just off the charts. And it just became irrelevant because she was pedaling more than you could count. It was more about distance—down the street and around the corner, working on turns.

And that was the whole second week, getting used to pavement and being safe and turning. Getting hand signals. At this point I also moved her up to a larger size of bike. I just went to Papa Wheelies bike shop—I told them what I was doing, and they gave me a bike. They gave it to Amy which I thought was great. I made a video of her thanking Papa Wheelies but she was very cool, didn't make eye contact. Didn't say much.

So we came to the bike trip. And she was amazing. She biked in the front of the pack, with confidence. About a mile and a half, some potholes and she did amazing and felt really good about it. And for the last two weeks, all of the fifth graders have this swagger—they are done with elementary school and moving on. And Amy had that swagger too—I think because of the bike.

A funny part of the story is that the computer teacher, whose room looks out over the back playground, had seen us and how great Amy was doing. And her daughter's in middle school, and in the new middle school there's this big banner, a photo of Amy at the head of a pack of kids, smiling, cycling across the new Portsmouth bridge when it opened after repairs—so she continued to bike.

After it was over, my principal, who knew this was going on, said this is how teaching should go in math, in reading, everything—meeting the student where they are.

There is so much here to admire: Ian's inventiveness in planning the bike ride to begin with, his attentiveness to Amy's hesitation, his careful calibration of the task of riding a bicycle (this is what we mean by scaffolding), his celebration of the incremental success she achieves, his awareness of the possibility of embarrassment in the learning, and his extraordinary commitment of time. Peter Johnston, in his classic text on teacher talk, *Choice Words* (2004), claims that we need to build a narrative of learning, of student agency, in our comments—which is exactly what Ian does, building in some graphing practice as a bonus.

The teaching gifts, the caring, on display in this story can't be reduced to a set of procedures, any more than Gatsby's smile can. But it seems to me there are some conversational practices that can create emotional space for students to take risks, speak out, and find their voice. But conventional classroom participation practices keep many students silent.

The Blank Turn

There is an old Shaker saying: "Never miss an opportunity to keep your mouth shut." Good advice for us teachers, I think, because it is well documented that we talk too much. When students do speak, there is often a recitation pattern that goes like this: (1) teacher asks question; (2) student is recognized by the teacher; (3) student answers; (4) teacher evaluates the answer of the student. Then on to the next question, the next student. The proportions are pretty obvious—even when students are raising their hands to respond (not always the case), the teacher has two out of every three turns. In the worst cases, when no student wants to answer, we end up channeling Ben Stein in *Ferris Bueller's Day Off* ("Anyone? Anyone?") and answer our own questions. As teachers we fall into this recitation pattern so easily. I know I do. It is the "default" setting in classroom talk.

So what is wrong with this picture? This pattern works if the purpose of classroom talk is to have students display fully formulated responses—and to be judged by the teacher. It works if classroom "discussion" is a form of recitation. But it doesn't work if the purpose of talk is to develop a real response. It can *convey* understanding or grasp of a fact, but can't *create* understanding—or community for that matter.

How many of us, after all, say what we really want to say on the first try? Rather, exploratory talk loops back again and again, as we formulate a thought, refine it, extend it, complicate it. It's messy. And we usually do this exploration in the presence of a sympathetic and interested audience who is not pressed for time. In this inviting space, our memory seems to work better—details are recalled, stories and other points of view mysteriously become available. That's the gift of talk.

The first thing we need to do as teachers is to realize that it is not about us. Maybe we all harbor, somewhere, that model of the brilliant, charismatic teacher, one who is dazzling and eloquent and impressive. But teaching, I am convinced, is not about us being brilliant, it is about students being brilliant. It's about them, after all. And the only way they can do this is if we give that generous gift of time and receptivity. There is an ancient saying, attributed to Cicero, that translates: "For those who want to learn, the obstacle can often be the authority of those who teach" (in Montaigne 1987, 169). Molly Tetreault, the writing center director at the University of New Hampshire, revealingly translates this principle into her own work with students:

> When I get on a roll on something, I can speak very articulately, especially when you've talked about some writing issue a lot. You can really speak to that topic—and you sound like you have great ideas and you really know what you are talking about. And I'm really careful about falling into that. The "ums" and the stumbles and the false starts and the reformulations—that's OK to have in a conference. It shows the student I am a human being and I don't have all the answers.

This tentativeness creates space for a conversational relationship—it invites participation and not dependency. There are few generalizations that hold for all good teachers, but I will hazard this one: Good teachers never appear rushed. Or make students feel rushed.

We can break this typical pattern with what I call the *blank turn*—a refusal to evaluate the student response and go to the next student. It sounds like this: "Say more about that." Or this: "Yes, go on." Or like this . . . just silence. Sometimes the student apologizes—"Boy, I'm just rambling on." And, if I'm on my game, I say, "Keep rambling."

Particularly as a writing teacher, I need students to hear what hasn't been written. It's pointless to write "expand this" or "more detail" if the student doesn't hear the detail he or she might add. (My colleague Mike Anderson even takes notes to keep a record of what students say.) They need this second text, the alternative story that they create orally. Then and only then can they see how the written one could be different.

This doesn't go on forever. Given time constraints it can't. But after a stretch of freetalk on the part of the students, I can enter in and reflect back what I have heard. Is there a new idea, a new focus, new details that might be included in the paper? If we are talking about a big project ahead, what directions seem promising, exciting to the writer? A colleague of mine has a variation when she gets the inevitable "I don't know" in answer to a question. She responds, "I know you don't know, honey, but if you did what would you say?" It feels like nonsense but it works!

Kenny Rotner, a primary care physician I interviewed, used a similar approach when conducting physicals:

> If you go to a doctor for a physical, so many doctors ask, "Is anything wrong?" A generic question. And most of the time people say "no." But I meticulously run down a set of questions. I troubleshoot. "Any difficulty sleeping? Periods of severe anxiety?" It opens doors that would be closed. It conveys to the patient that I want to know. And you can't rush it. If you convey that you are in a rush—if you don't make eye contact, you're not sitting down, you're going to inhibit openness.

It sounds easy, but listening and waiting can be hard work. Harder than talking. Talking, after all, is a form of self-stimulation. When I am tired I tend to overtalk, create brilliant minilectures, digress into personal experience, as the student sinks into silence and passivity.

So in this age of high tech and expensive programs, let me offer up this simple and powerful intervention—the blank turn. It costs us nothing but our attention. It is built on the rock solid principle that we need talk, and a receptive audience, to build understanding, to know what we know. In Bernard Pomerance's play, *The Elephant Man*, the deformed main character, Merrick, has the experience of being listened to for the first time—and he finds he can speak: "Before I spoke with people, I did not think of those things because there was no one to think them for. But now things come out of my mouth that are true" (1977).

Anchoring

One major theme in the studies of human biases is our tendency to economize effort. As much as we need novelty and surprise, our first instinct is economical, to fit any new experience into a preexisting slot, or pattern, or schema, or stereotype. Novelty takes work, as does real listening. In his book, *How Doctors Think* (2007), Jerome Groopman analyzes the shortcuts doctors take in diagnosis, especially when they are under time pressure.

One especially pernicious economizing practice is "anchoring." Imagine an overweight African American woman comes into a doctor's office and complains about numbness in her feet. The doctor instantly decides on the diagnosis of diabetes and on a sequence of tests and treatments. It is instantaneous, and he or she may be right. But this anchoring precludes alternatives (multiple sclerosis, for example), and it may mean that any conversation leads only to a confirmation of this initial impression. This bias may also preclude any openings to listen to the woman's feelings about her condition—her attitude toward her own illness. It is easy to imagine how a doctor, on the clock to see twenty-five patients in a day, will do this. (One of Groopman's suggestions is for the patient to take an active role to disrupt this automatic tendency—asking, for example, could it be something else, is there an alternative treatment. Not an easy role for everyone.)

I believe that this tendency, to anchor, is a danger for any diagnostic profession, including, for sure, teaching. A student hands in a paper that seems to ramble without a clear focus—but with my eagle eyes I can see a possible thesis on page 3, and I am primed to offer up this revision possibility. I'm ready! But if I am on my game, I try to get the student's sense of his own paper, and it turns out that he really *liked* writing it. Interesting. I ask, "What did you like about writing it?" And we're off on a real discussion, far more meaningful for both of us, than me sharing my brilliant insight. We may get to my thesis suggestion, but better if we can unpack his *liking* comment.

An entire specialty of medicine, narrative medicine, has emerged to help physicians become better listeners by "honoring the stories of illness." Rita Charon, a leader in this field, writes movingly about how this listening process works. In one case, she treats a forty-six-year-old Dominican man with shortness of breath and chest pain.

> I say to him at the start of our first visit, "I will be your doctor, so I have to learn a great deal about your body and your health and your life. Please tell me what you think I should know about your situation." And then I do my best not to say a word, to not write on the medical chart, but to absorb what he emits about himself—about his health concerns, his family, his work his fears, and his hopes. I listen not only for the content of the narrative but also its form—its temporal course, its images, its associated subplots, its silences, where he chooses to begin telling of

> himself, how he sequences symptoms with other life events. After a few minutes, the patient stops talking and begins to weep. I ask him why he cries. He says, "No one ever let me do this before." (2006, 177)

If we are honest with ourselves, we will admit that it is nearly—nearly—impossible to comprehend someone else's reality. We may say, "I know how you feel"—but we really don't. And often we don't try hard enough; we short-circuit. Perhaps the best we can do is to invite stories, of illness, of writing, of reading—to ask, "What is it like to be you?"

Uptake

In a description of being the "silent" student, one of my students likened her minimal contribution, at the very end of the class, to the closing music of a movie that no one listens to as they leave the theatre. The movie fades out, and so does she. It is the very nature of sound to be momentary, vibrations of air that vanish almost as they are produced—echoes fascinate us because they prolong or double the sounds we make. In a conversation, few things are as disheartening as this momentariness, the sense that whatever we say gets lost, that it doesn't register with others, is forgotten. The so-called discussion moves forward as if we hadn't spoken—or worst of all, there is a deadly pause, and no one knows how to respond to what has been said. Just a few seconds of this awkward silence is enough to silence a lot of us. We feel that what we have said is so inappropriate, so ill considered, so crude, so stupid, so out of place that it defies response.

The antidote to the ephemeral quality of talk is uptake—the way respondents build on, echo, extend a previous comment, a practice that begins in infancy, even before the child is speaking actual words. Recent research suggests that language development is enhanced by "contingent" talk patterns, sometimes referred to as "parentese" but more commonly known as baby talk. A baby drops her rattle and gestures toward it, verbalizing an "ah, ah" (I want that back); the caretaker, using a distinctive higher pitch, slower tempo, and exaggerated contours,

The antidote to the ephemeral quality of talk is uptake—the way respondents build on, echo, extend a previous comment, a practice that begins in infancy, even before the child is speaking actual words.

says, "Does baby want her rattle? Here is baby's rattle." Once the rattle is returned the baby might verbalize an expression of pleasure as she grabs it. These interactions are sometimes referred to as "serve and volley"—the child serves (drops the toy), the caretaker volleys—and the game is on. Researchers have found that these contingent responses are associated with increased vocalization, new phonetic forms, and enhanced language development. In other words it is not the sheer volume of talk the child hears, but the linking of volley to serve that may be most significant (Ramirez-Esparza, Garcia-Sierra, and Kuhl 2014).

The significance of uptake for classroom instruction has been demonstrated by Martin Nystrand and Adam Gamoran in their research on classroom talk. It may be as simple as a follow-up question as in this example they cite:

Teacher: What does Odysseus want to do there?

Student: Make friends and get food.

Teacher: Why make friends? (Nystrand and Gamoran 1991, 264)

The student comment is not lost; rather, it forms the basis for the next question the teacher asks. It is "taken up." That uptake creates coherence, depth, and ultimately a greater capacity for reading and writing about literature. It's not hard to see why. As Vygotsky (1978) has famously claimed, our thought processes begin in conversation, in the social give-and-take of talk—and are subsequently internalized as "individual" thought. Uptake is a demonstration of connectiveness, of how an idea is developed, defended, explained, tested, challenged; immersion in a culture of uptake allows the learner to internalize the moves necessary for fluent analytic writing.

Uptake happens so naturally in many of our conversations that one would expect it to be the norm of classroom discussions. But that is not the case. Particularly in lower tracks, "discussions" are typically nonconsecutive questions, actually display questions (the teacher knows the answer) posed in the time honored question-answer-evaluate pattern. It is recitation, not discussion. Only in the upper tracks did Nystrand and Gamoran find more authentic conversation and uptake, and even there it was rare.

Not only is uptake critical for developing analytic fluency—it is a critically important collaborative skill in its own right. To put it simply—conversational partners skilled at uptake make us feel smart, make us feel fluent. We may not be aware of how this occurs in a linguistic sense, but conversation seems to flow when they are around. We feel attended to, and our comments matter. I also think that good listeners, those who build on what we say, invite us to be a good listener building on what they say—it's reciprocal.

The practice of uptake can be modeled and taught. Mike Anderson, who for years worked as a curriculum leader for the Responsive Classroom, has thought deeply about student talk, and he challenges teachers to be deliberate and explicit in teaching students to converse. "When you really start to break down the skills, the behaviors that people enlist in really rich conversations, it's unbelievable how many there are and how complex they are." He works with teachers to create a four-stage scaffolded model of instruction: (1) stating the purpose and importance of the skill being taught, (2) providing a high-quality example of that skill, (3) facilitating guided practice in using the skill, and (4) allowing for independent practice.

I asked him for an example of how this might be used to teach uptake in the morning meetings that are such a basic anchor in the Responsive Classroom approach. I'll let him take it from here.

> Suppose the focus is on building coherent conversations about social stories (not the writing) like visiting a grandmother—the kind of sharing that goes on in Morning Meeting. As we all know there is a tendency for students (and adults too) to say, "That reminds me . . ." and the focus shifts to them.
>
> I'll begin by stating that the goal is to make comments about someone else's story that keeps the focus on the teller. Then I might start with my own story about playing Monopoly with my son. After the story we will brainstorm sentence openings that keep the focus on the teller's story:
>
> - You must have . . .
> - It sounds like you . . .
> - I wonder if you . . .
>
> Then we try some of these in class. A student might say, "It sounds like you had fun playing Monopoly with your son." And I might say, "Yeah we hung out for a couple of hours." For several days we work on having students make these kinds of teller-focused comments.
>
> We would use the same process with framing questions, and here the goal would be to pose genuine questions. Too often, especially in writer's workshop, questions can become formulaic (e.g., "What's your favorite part?"). So we will begin by discussing the characteristics of a good elaborative question, one you are curious about. If a student tells the story

of breaking his finger, for example, a good question might be: "Was it on you writing hand?" and if so, "How are you doing your writing?" Something focused on the specific story. Once these skills are in place for the told stories of students, we bridge to using them in writing conferences.

We simply cannot learn the tremendous range of conversational skills through this deliberate process—many are learned tacitly, particularly if they are part of the fabric of family talk. But it is also true that many—I would wager most—of the mistakes we make as teachers involve "assumptive teaching." We assume students know how to engage in processes, and that all we have to do is ask that it be done. For example, we ask students to discuss a passage from a book in small groups. But what does that "discuss" entail; what steps are we expecting them to take in discussing? Do we want to have them identify what they see as a key word, a key sentence, a section that confuses them? (And what do we mean by *key*?) And if so, what is the next step? To avoid assumptive teaching we need to follow Mike Anderson's lead and surgically examine seeming simple and habitual processes.

At the end of my interview with Mike, he showed me a video of this process in action: a first-grade teacher modeling how to choose a reading buddy. She went through his four-stage sequence. I know my own tendency would be to be assumptive, to assume that this would be an automatic and simple task. But it is easy to imagine, once I thought about it, that the language of request (as opposed to "be my reading buddy!") might not be automatic.

One extremely valuable skill is *referencing prior comments*—to indicate agreement or disagreement (and how to do that respectfully), or to provide an example of a point made earlier, additional evidence for a statement made earlier, an additional explanation. Students make specific reference and name or summarize the comments made by another student in the class. "I can see how Jonathan sees this character as mean, but it seems to me there are times when he at least tries to help others. Like when . . ." Anderson calls this using "soft language"—disagreeing without being disagreeable. By *soft language*, he means what linguists call "hedging"—perhaps using the conditional tense ("Another way we *might* look at it is . . ."; "The advantage of this approach *could be* . . .") or to concede virtues to the view you are challenging ("I can see that doing *x*, will help us. . . . But *y* might even be more effective in . . ."). There is, to be sure, the opposite danger of seeming too tentative (or insincere), but students won't be welcome in deliberative discussions if they have none of these tools. Unfortunately a dominant media model is discussion as battle, with talking heads trying to score points and win, hardly the kind of situation to invite participation from reluctant students.

One strategy I love to use is the *hypothetical other.* I often bring in accounts of ethical dilemmas into the classroom, inspired by Michael Sandel's Justice course at Harvard. The Ethicist column of the *New York Times* magazine is a good source. One of my favorite dilemmas is this one:

> When I checked into a hotel in California, I was starving, so I ate the $6 box of Oreos from the minibar. Later that day, I walked down the street to a convenience store, bought an identical box for $2.50 and replenished the minibar before the hotel had a chance to restock it. Was this proper? My view is "no harm, no foul." In fact, my box was fresher: the Oreos I ate were going to expire three months before the box I replaced them with. (Cohen 2010)

The first reactions among about any group I share this with would be—sure, "no harm, no foul." The situation remains unchanged with the replacement, possibly even improved. Besides, these minibars are a rip-off.

I don't personally argue against this consensus; I don't pit my view against theirs, but I do bring in another contesting voice, something like this: "Suppose the hotel manager said that if everyone did this, there would be no revenue from the service and it would have to be discontinued for everyone." Or, "We are counting on that revenue from the minibar, and if we don't get it, we would have to make it up in slightly higher room rates." Or, "But we are selling not simply the cookies, but a service—which you took advantage of, but didn't pay for. That, in our view, is stealing." I don't want to get in a position when I am arguing my view against theirs—but wherever they are, I try to be someplace different, bringing in a voice that pushes them to consider an alternative. A colleague of mine calls this "counterdiscourse."

I try to make this talk playful, hypothetical, nonconfrontational—and in fact, for me critical thinking is a form of play. Watch an infant, a one-year-old for example, with some object: a rattle, a block, a plastic hammer. The child tests it out—throws it, drops it, shakes it, tastes it, hits other objects to see what sound it makes, makes marks on it, pretends it is something else. That's what we want students to do with ideas. What happens when one idea hits another, when it is turned upside down? How well does it hold up when we shake it?

Teachers can also show soft hands by generously summarizing. I wince when I see summarization treated as a low-level cognitive skill because it is so crucial in effective collaboration. One way to show that a contribution has been heard is to reflect it back to the speaker or writer, and to do so in a way that conveys the significance of the effort. In writing conferences I try (when I am on my game) to articulate what the writer is trying to do—"In this paper I see you showing the effect this teacher of yours, Mr. MacFarlane, had on you, and you do that by showing a central example of him helping you when you were struggling with algebra [here I might read a section of the paper], and you really show your feeling by slowing down the scene where you hear the news of his death, and when you are speaking at his memorial service." Something like that. Peter Johnston associates this move with the question: "Let's see if I got this right?"

That's what we want students to do with ideas. What happens when one idea hits another, when it is turned upside down? How well does it hold up when we shake it?

I try to convey a basic message: I get it. I am on board with your effort. Again, when we are in a hurry we may skip this step and jump to questions or suggestions for change before the writer is convinced he or she is understood. In the conference model developed by the great Donald Graves, he emphasized "receiving" the piece of writing, acknowledging what has been heard. This before any questions.

A related feature of high-quality instruction is the *authentic question*, one for which the answer is not known—and again these were distressingly rare and skewed toward the upper tracks. The more common form is the *display question*—where the expected answer is known by the teacher. Not only does the authentic question help break out of the recitation script, it gratifies us to know that someone is curious about us.

I had good models of questioning (and listening) in my own family when I was growing up. It was soon after World War II and no one had much money in our small town. Entertainment was visiting each other's homes, usually unannounced. Our home was filled with stories, of the war, of events at the local college where my dad taught, of the stupidity of Republicans. My dad's best friend Dick Snyder was the best. He would take a position in an easy chair, lean forward, and perhaps tell the story of a football player for the University of Indiana who lost an eye in the war. Normally he had a glass eye—but when he was playing, he took the eye out so that the lineman across from him would stare into an empty socket, like playing against Cyclops. I loved those stories.

My parents were not the tellers, but the audience. At the time they seemed passive and less talented than the great storytellers who stopped by. Only later, I'm embarrassed to admit, did I understand how they helped create these stories, how they brought them out with their questions and genuine curiosity. How they listened. I belatedly figured out why they were such popular hosts. I had missed all those vital cues.

Again Peter Johnston's *Choice Words* (2004) and *Opening Minds* (2012) are invaluable guides to the authentic questioning. A major theme of both books is the idea of *process*, for my money the most empowering idea in instruction. Without the belief in process, that we can act on a deliberate plan of short steps to get us where we want to go—without that idea we fall victim to a set of debilitating myths. Success (and failure) becomes a product of magic, or inspiration, or talent, or chance, none of which we can shape or even guide. These myths can lead to passivity, even a feeling of helplessness. But a robust faith in processes of learning allows us to manage difficulty and be alert to the often microscopic advances we or our students make.

For Peter Johnston, learning is shaped—enhanced or restricted—by the kinds of story we tell about ourselves as learners. If we see learning as limited by fixed attributes ("I'm not a math person"), we tell one kind of story. But if we tell a story of process, of learning by engaging in a manageable set of steps that we can plan and control, we tell a very different story, what Johnston calls an "agentive story," one where the learner is the agent, controlling the process. A number of the teacher questions he recommends push the student to be this agent:

- "How did you figure that out?"
- "What problems did you come across today?"
- "Where are you going with this piece of writing?"
- "How are you planning to go about this?"
- "What are you noticing?"
- "You managed to figure that out with each other's help. How did you do that?"

However gentle and attentive our questioning is, however much space we give, I am convinced that we need to frequently shift from an interrogative mode to a narrative mode—we need to open the class up to *stories*. In a classroom, as in writing, a story does many things. It makes for personal disclosure, helping everyone to know classmates (and the teacher) better—it humanizes. It creates a climate of cognitive ease; we don't have to struggle to make logical connections because the flow of a story is familiar. Studies show we use less glucose when do this kinds of thinking (Kahneman 2011, 43). It puts the teller—and not the teacher—at the center. And whatever abstractions or theories or ideas we might be dealing with, we are grounded in the particular and familiar. Jesus knew this. And so did Abraham Lincoln.

In the movie *Lincoln*, at a time when he and members of his cabinet are tensely waiting for news about the shelling of Wilmington, Lincoln blurts out, "Come out you old rat," which is a line spoken by Ethan Allen as he stormed Fort Ticonderoga during the Revolutionary War. Stanton, Lincoln's Secretary of War, can see what is coming: "No! No, you're, you're going to tell a story! I don't believe that I can bear to listen to another one of your stories right now!"

Undeterred, Lincoln tells the story about Allen visiting England after the war to conduct business with the king. At one dinner, he drinks a good deal and he needs to go to the privy, where he finds a picture of George Washington displayed. He doesn't mention the picture when he returns, but the curious host finally asks him if he had seen Washington's picture:

> He had. Well, what did he think of its placement, did it seem appropriately located to Mr. Allen? Mr. Allen said it did. His host was astounded! Appropriate? George Washington's likeness in a water closet? Yes, said Mr. Allen, where it'll do good service: the whole world knows nothing'll make an Englishman shit quicker than the sight of George Washington. (Kushner 2011)

Lincoln's story eases the tension of the moment, but it also subtly links it to earlier military victories and the colonies' ascendency over the British. It injects confidence into a moment of deep national uncertainty.

Intermission I—A Reflection on Failure

Failure is hip now. We are regularly advised to "embrace failure." One of my heroes, Don Murray, would regularly tell the writing tribe he advised: "Failure is instructive. It's your successes you have to worry about." In other words, your successes can keep you locked in an unchanging pattern of behavior; only failure can cause you to break out of it. We need what Piaget (or John Dewey) might call the *disequilibrium of failure* to have true learning take place.

Statements like these, which become repeated mantras, should be treated, I think, like engine parts: after so many miles (or repetitions) they should be inspected and perhaps replaced. So here goes. To begin: when I hear this praise of failure, it usually comes from people that seem largely successful. Murray was a successful columnist and a Pulitzer Prize winner before he was thirty. By contrast, my wife works as a guardian ad litem for children in the court system—children of abusive and severely dysfunctional parents, who are mired in failure: addictions, inability to hold jobs, evictions, violence, petty crime, even inability to afford a working car. Failure to these parents is not some welcome opportunity for growth, it is a heavy and discouraging weight they carry daily. It is failure unrelated to any success.

When people praise failure, I believe they are praising provisional failure, setbacks in a story that generally ends well. Daniel Kahneman (2011) describes several clever experiments that demonstrate the significance of end points—that our "takeaway," our memory, of an experience is fundamentally related to the way it ends. Or as Shakespeare put it, "All's well that ends well."

Some of these experiments involve holding your hand in uncomfortably cold water—and rating the pain of the experience. In one treatment the subjects held their hand in cold (fifty-seven degrees) water for sixty seconds, and then were offered a warm towel. In the other treatment, the subject kept the hand in the water for ninety seconds, but for the last thirty seconds the temperature rose by one degree—just enough to experience a slight lessening of pain. Subjects were then asked which of the two treatments they would prefer for a third trial (which didn't happen—the point was to test the way they evaluated the two versions).

Logically, we would expect the majority to prefer the shorter treatment because the duration of discomfort is shorter. But in fact, 80 percent chose the ninety-second treatment—even though it involved thirty additional seconds of discomfort. The end point (the sensation of gradual warming) is critical in the way we remember the experience, seemingly canceling out the longer duration of discomfort. In the same way, I propose, when failure is provisional, in the midpoint but not the end state, we minimize it in our memory. Kahneman calls this tendency "the tyranny of the remembering self."

I have seen my own memory play this trick on me with difficult hikes in the White Mountains—what stays with me is the gratification of a successful hike: the memory of the difficult parts (e.g., the difficult descent on the Lion's Head ridge of Mount Washington), the real discomfort, is minimized. But when I redo some of these hikes (some of which I have done multiple times), I am positively shocked at how hard they are. Another classic example is the memory women have of successful childbirth!

It follows that if we (or our students) can view failure as a provisional way station on the way to some positive result, the very pain of that failure recedes from our memory. And I think we intuitively know that when we treat painful experiences as learning lessons or tests that make us stronger, or teach us something important, and when we wrap them in the narrative of self-development and personal progress. Unless we can plausibly do that, we are left with an unedifying experience, another setback, a mark of futility. That kind of failure is not something anyone wants to embrace.

It follows that a mindset that values perseverance and process is a necessary but not sufficient prerequisite for effective learning. We all need conditions where these traits take us somewhere, where there is some form of success that, like alchemy, transforms frustration and difficulty into what Peter Johnston calls an "agentive narrative," a story in which we are the hero. It takes coaching: the setting of goals and appropriately difficult challenges—and the gift of witnessing and communicating small successes. Absent these conditions, this support, this wisdom, we have no reason to value failure. And to the extent that we create a learning history of overcoming difficulty, we build learning capital that we can draw on when we face difficult challenges.

I am also convinced that creating these better stories cannot be a purely individual effort. My brother, who has gone through a tough divorce and depression, not to mention bruising battles with the IRS, has this motto: "We all need a team." We can't do it alone. There are too many psychological holes we can fall into. We lose perspective too easily, exaggerate failure too readily. And even when we are introspective and reflective, we are hearing voices from our past.

As we engage in processes of learning and build a history, we can revert to that history in times of difficulty. As I write now (October 26, 2015), I feel so uncertain about this "book" (in quotes because it seems so presumptuous to expose this word without them). I am not sure where or if this chapter fits, and, as always, the prospect of holding together an entire book is still scary to me. (The fact that you are now reading this as a book shows I made it, but I don't feel that now.)

I can take comfort and courage from the fact that I have been here before. I have had these same doubts before and worked through them. I replay the line from Theodore Roethke's great poem "The Waking" (1953): "I learn by going where I have to go." I have faith that by getting to my desk each day, writing my 500 words, I can find my way. The process of writing will teach me what I need to do. It has in the past. If students can consciously engage in a process, and build a history of working through difficulty and complexity, that history becomes capital that they can draw on.

Intermission II: In Praise of Praise

The subject of praise—its inevitability and misuse—has been a subject of discussion for centuries, though the term *flattery* was more commonly used. Machiavelli called it a "plague." The tragedy of *King Lear* is set in motion by the aging king's need for flattery and his two false daughters, Goneril and Regan, pile it on:

> **Goneril:** Sir, I love you more than words can wield the matter;
> Dearer than eyesight, space and liberty;
> Beyond what can be valued, rich or rare . . . (I. 1 55–57)

Regan chimes in that she loves him all of this and more, that she is only happy ("felicitate") in her father's love—provoking the more honest youngest daughter Cordelia to ask how her sisters could marry if all their love went to their father. Her refusal to flatter in this way seals her disinheritance (Lear calls her "my sometime daughter"). A warning from his honest counselor, the Earl of Kent, about what happens when "power to flattery bows" leads to his dismissal as well.

The historic concern about flattery focused on the way it could corrupt the decision-making of those in power; and our concern is the reverse, the ways those in authority use it with students. But the issues remain the same—the susceptibility to praise, the potential for manipulation, the problem of insincerity, and a dependence on praise that inhibits honest self-appraisal or criticism. The great educational iconoclast Alfie Kohn (2001) (with whom I usually agree) takes perhaps the most austere line. He, and other critics, see these problems:

- Praise is built on a power relationship, with the teacher in power.
- Regular praise builds a habit of needing praise—it can become an addiction.
- The gratification of learning should come from learning itself and not from outside praise.

- Praise is often used, cynically or not, as a means of controlling behavior ("Look how quietly Adam is sitting in his seat").
- Praise, particularly global praise ("You're a great writer") provides no useful information for improvement and can even inhibit risk-taking because the learner doesn't want to put this identity in danger. In effect, it reinforces a fixed mindset in which competence is seen as something you "have" (or don't have), not something developed through persistence and engaging in a process.
- Praise should focus on persistence and hard work, rather than these global and fixed traits.

We might add to this list the embarrassment factor—especially when the praise is overdone.

Kohn leaves the door ajar, slightly, for comments that provide information or observation, perhaps even noting improvement, but in general he sees praise as the characteristic of an unhealthy and imbalanced teacher-student relationship.

Carol Dweck is clearly a driving force in the reimagining of praise, and she cites numerous studies that show the negative effects of global praise that focuses on intelligence or abilities: often a slight rewording of an assignment or direction had a major impact on performance in controlled studies. Like many educators who have read her work, I have had to deal with my own cognitive dissonance, because I see many of my own tendencies described as ineffective and inhibiting. What's more, I see my own history as a learner, or the way I tell it, called into question—because there were times, critical times, when I was praised by people I admire—and it made, and in recollection still makes, a huge difference. In moments of discouragement, I revisit that praise.

I am not unique here. In an interview with Terry Gross, the singer-songwriter Iris DeMent describes the effect one of her teachers had on her (NPR Music 2015). Though she had a rich background singing in the Pentecostal church, DeMent didn't begin songwriting until she was twenty-five. A major turning point was taking a first-year writing class at Washburn University in Topeka, Kansas, after she had been out of school since she dropped out in tenth grade:

> I had this wonderful English Composition teacher. It was my dream to write stories. She would give us this assignment to write stories and my grammar was a mess and my spelling was bad. And she would write

> these beautiful notes every time I turned in these stories (pause as she chokes up). She was so *kind* to me. Just simple little teacher notes, you know. But her red pen—she'd say these really kind things. "You have imagination." And it encouraged me. She didn't criticize me about what I didn't know how to do. And I just sank myself into that class . . . A door just flew open after that.

DeMent herself probably cannot vouch for the exact wording of these teacher notes, but it is significant that she remembers a global comment "you have imagination"—exactly the form of praise we are being cautioned to avoid.

Another example, this one from my own childhood. When my brother was about nine and playing minor league baseball, he mishandled a ball at first base—it bounced up and broke his nose. After the visit to the doctor, Dad reassured him, "You're a good first baseman." This became a mantra in our family, repeated after any baseball game, good fielding or bad: "You're a good first baseman." It morphed into a general statement about dealing with any problem. When my brother had problems with his business: "You're a good first baseman." When he went through an excruciating divorce: "You're a good first baseman." It conveyed his confidence that whatever difficulty came my brother's way, he could handle it because of his core abilities. Dad used it right up to his death. And in a sense the mantra has outlived him, because my brother still invokes it for himself.

Finally, from my own teaching. I recently had dinner with a former student who has since become a literacy specialist, activist, and educational writer. The conversation turned to the comments we write on papers and how powerful (for good and ill) they can be. She said, "I remember one comment you wrote on my paper." (And I'm thinking, "Please God, I hope it wasn't an insensitive one!") She continued, "I sometimes go back and reread it when I need encouragement. You wrote in the margin, 'You write like a dream.'"

Three global acts of praise. Three violations of the rules.

Praise, as it is offered in real settings, defies the rules currently being promulgated, the linguistic formulations about what is "good" and "bad." In actual relationships so much depends on timing, relationship, intention, tone, gesture, and the personal codes we develop. Affirming a positive fixed trait—such as DeMent's "imagination"—does not necessarily promote caution or a lack of risk-taking; in her case it did exactly the opposite. It can be empowering to imagine that we have stable traits or aptitudes, deeply rooted in our temperament, that are *ours* and that we can call on in times of crisis or challenge.

It also seems to me naive to imagine that you can sanitize the teacher-student relationship so the power dynamic vanishes—and the student is working purely autonomously. As learners, we accept, to some degree, the authority of the teacher and trust that he or she will take us where we want to go. In a parallel way, a teacher's sense of efficacy and self-worth is tied up in the achievement of students—so it is natural, inevitable, that teachers celebrate the successes of students, and that students value, even cherish, these celebrations. This power dynamic can become dysfunctional: when the wrong kinds of achievement—like compliance—are celebrated, or when praise is "lazy," merely habitual, or when praise is not balanced with constructive criticism. But these possibilities do not lead to the conclusion that teachers should divest authority—as if we could.

In one of his great essays on teaching writing, Peter Elbow (1993) makes the unconventional claim that the most instructive form of assessment we can make is *liking*, which rings true to me. I'm often surprised by people who commiserate with me about the fact that I teach the first-year writing classes—like it must feel awful to have to read through that stuff, what a martyr. They're vaguely disappointed, and unconvinced, when I say I like a lot of the writing I get; I enjoy reading it. This is true because I look for things to like, legitimately like.

As Elbow describes it, "liking" is not a mushy, subjective, sentimental means to promote self-esteem, but a precise tool for helping students to internalize a set of standards, to gain a sense of how writing works. In almost any paper, there is something to like: a word choice, an image, a bit of humor, a good detail, a sharp verb, a telling fact or statistic, a fine bit of logic. There is something that engages me as a reader, and I share that response with the writer. The initial message is not "This is a problem, correct it," but "*This* is good, do more of this." And I have found that if students believe that I am clearly alert to what is going well, they can listen to observations about what is not.

Sometimes that something to like is not even in the paper. Years ago, one of my writing students had written a paper about her hometown in Vermont. The paper was completely flat, factually accurate I am sure, but with nothing vivid or memorable. We talked about changes and didn't seem to be getting anywhere, when I noticed she had a postcard of Norman Rockwell's iconic painting of Rosie the Riveter.

"Oh that," she said. "That's my mother."

"Your mother was Rosie the Riveter!?"

"She posed for him when she was a young woman. In fact, he painted a lot of people in our town."

"Could you find them, interview them about what it was like, what Rockwell was like."

"Sure, I never thought of that. I'm going home for Thanksgiving."

The paper was great.

Sometimes I don't even have to make any comment, just read the student's words, but read them as literature, like Rion's description of a worn and beloved pair of boots:

> The uppers are scuffed from four years of abuse. They still have a dent on the toe from when I dropped a log on my foot. The sole, well, it is certainly the most worn part. The tread is very nearly gone, likely from the summer I spent working on a rough cement floor, though I have hardly been keeping track of the wear and tear. It is also cracked along the ball of my foot, allowing the boot to flex and move around my foot. In addition, the sole has split horizontally. However, super glue, and later, five-minute epoxy, have made it a nonissue. The laces are original, a dark brown, twisted and matted in the shape of what was once a knot, but is now a tangled nylon lock about my ankles. I have been lucky, because, with extreme care and diligence, I have worked to keep these shoes smell free, though it was a challenge.

I hope that simply reading it aloud to him was enough, that he could see how I appreciated not simply the detail but the way his boots held a story of his work life. It was my way of saying thanks.

When we demonstrate "liking," we are offering another important lesson—namely the necessity of generosity in the writing process. When we see teachers reading our work generously, we have a model to internalize, so that we can be generous toward ourselves. Not that we become complacent or protective of every precious word, but that we can be kind toward ourselves. We can accept ourselves, take pleasure in our own work, and not succumb to the trap of being hypercritical. This *self-generosity,* I am convinced, is crucial to staying engaged in writing—or any other challenging activity for that matter. It is great to have that internal critic who refuses to let us settle, but we need an internal cheerleader to balance that harsh voice.

Perhaps in a more perfect world we would not need this continual affirmation, we could be fearless, confident, willing to take on hard tasks with no need of support and encouragement. But think of that bicycle that Amy learned to ride—how improbable it is that those two thin tires could support a human body, that she could find a way to balance herself and move forward without falling. How many of us remember that moment, when someone said to us, "It's OK. Just get on the bike, put your feet on the ground, and push forward a few feet. Yes, yes, that's it."

III

EMBARRASSMENT AND THE THREE Rs

(CHAPTER 6)

Math Shame

Why Are We All on the Outside Looking In?

My shame was radical.

—**JANE KENYON,** "TROUBLE WITH MATH IN A ONE-ROOM COUNTRY SCHOOL"

I'm about to take you to a place you may want to avoid.

Today (November 18, 2015), while reading the *Boston Globe,* I came across some sample math questions on the current grade 8 *Massachusetts Comprehensive Assessment System* test. Here was one:

Solve the equation for x: $0.5\,(5 - 7x) = 8 - (4x + 6)$

I decided to give it a try. As I started to work on it, some old math feelings began to surface. One was irritation—when do we ever do calculations like this in "real life"? Because of problems like this I developed a personal dislike for the letter *x,* always wandering about, trying to find himself, and his coconspirator *y.* A psychologist friend of mine speculates that a dislike for these letters might be a wider cultural reaction.

But I started in and became entangled in negative numbers: what do you do when you "add" a negative number? I began to feel in my gut a very mild panic that I couldn't work this through, an eighth-grade problem. This shouldn't be hard for me.

With some effort I calmed myself and thought, *Hmm, I can get rid of that nasty .5 by multiplying both sides by 2*. So I get:

$$5 - 7x = 16 - (8x + 12)$$

This is looking better.

OK, I am getting annoyed at the parentheses. I decide to just get rid of them—but I'm not sure of that. So:

$$5 - 7x = 16 - 8x - 12$$

(Because the minus sign applies to everything in parentheses, I hope.)

I subtract the 12 from the 16 and get:

$$5 - 7x = 4 - 8x$$

(Looking better.)

What if I add $8x$ to each side? After all you could add a pet dog to each side, and it would be OK if it was exactly the same pet dog. It would still be equal.

$$5 + x = 4$$

Subtract 5 from each side:

$$x = -1$$

I got it right. I can make it, maybe, in eighth grade.

Are you still there, reader?

When I mentioned the title of this chapter, "Math Shame," to a fellow editor, she replied, "Actually I feel no shame at all. I'm just not good at math and I'm fine with that." There is probably no other major, required subject area, that we so regularly divide into the haves and have-nots—the ones good at math and then the rest of us. Math class is the motherland of the fixed mindset. For most of us, math never becomes a language, something that we can be fluent in. I suspect that for proficient math students equations must feel like sentences, as if there is a ready and seemingly natural syntax at their disposal.

But for the rest of us, problems like the one above take us back to an emotional space that we thought we had escaped. It brings up a queasy feeling that one friend called "post-traumatic math syndrome." And lest this comparison seem overblown, an Iraq veteran, interviewed by a graduate student I advise, compared the emotions he experienced in his college math course to ones he felt in combat.

As I worked through this problem, a couple things stood out for me. One: I could never have done the problem if I was under time pressure. It is common on tests to give no more than ninety seconds to an equation like this. That limit would have fried me. And two: even on such a basic problem, I had to calm myself, to fight back a small panic or frustration, especially when I bravely killed off those parentheses. It's like my history of math class was always threatening to come back to discourage me. My memory of such problems is that I would create some stupid and careless error along the way—almost a sure thing if I had to do a lot of them.

As I noted earlier, time pressure is a key feature of the anxiety we face—to the point where we feel penalized for being deliberate. There is a research basis for this feeling of being penalized—called the "processing efficiency theory" (Eysenck and Calvo 1992), which is summarized this way:

> The intrusive thoughts and worry characteristics of high anxiety are thought to compete with the ongoing cognitive task for the limited resources of working memory. The result of such competition is either a slowing of performance or a decline in accuracy—in other words, lower cognitive efficiency. Because high-anxiety individuals must expend greater cognitive effort to attain the same level of performance achieved by low-anxiety individuals, processing efficiency is lower for high-anxiety individuals. (Ashcraft and Kirk 2001, 225)

This makes perfect sense to me. Although I may not qualify as "high anxiety" in math, I did need to slow down and calm myself, the classic "take a deep breath," as I did the problem. It is easy to imagine a compounding effect of such pauses on a timed test. Because I slowed down, I could put myself at risk for not finishing, and *that* concern was an additional intrusion, a drain on working memory. At that point there might be three demands on my cognitive capacity—the task of solving the problem, the anxiety of doing this math, and the concern about moving fast enough through the test.

Filling a Tub with a Hole in It

So let's move up the scale to a problem on the Preliminary SAT (PSAT) that might be taken by tenth graders:

> A 19-liter measure consists by volume of 1 part juice and 18 parts water. If x liters of juice and y liters of water are added to the

> mixture to make a 54 liter mixture consisting by volume of one part juice to two parts water, what is the value of x? (in Hacker 2016, 74)

That's a lot of information in each sentence! I had to reread it several times to get my bearings.

At first I was thrown off by the language and situation. What in hell is a "19-liter measure"? It is hard to visualize a *measure.* I also worry about repeated use of *by volume*. Was this some special thing I should be paying attention to—aren't liters volume? I'm distracted by this language. And why have the test writers chosen to write in the passive voice, when we know that sentences are more comprehensible when there is an agent doing something—perhaps the most basic principle of comprehension. Finally the whole situation feels artificial—to create a mixture you usually start out with the two ingredients separate, not something partially mixed. (Not to be picky, but what would be the purpose of creating such a watery drink?)

Enough grousing.

I started off by trying to imagine this change—the mixture I thought would get a lot juicier at 1:2. I also calculated the total amount of juice to be added to the mixture (35 liters: 54 – 19) but that didn't seem to be much help. So I calculated how much juice would be *in* the final mixture. If the ratio was 1:2, juice to water, the juice would be $\frac{1}{3}$ of the final mixture—or 18 liters. Now the answer appeared easy: you would have to add 17 liters of juice to get the right mixture.

Only one problem. It took me four minutes and twenty-nine seconds to do this—and the time allotted was seventy-nine seconds. I would be in deep trouble.

This mixture problem is also an example of pseudo story problems—lame attempts to make a problem realistic—that at times approach parody, as in this widely ridiculed example:

> Kachima is making triangular bandanas for the dogs and cats in her pet club. The base of the bandana is the length of the collar with 4 inches added to each end to tie it on. The height is $\frac{1}{2}$ of the collar length. If Kachima's dog has a collar length of 12 inches, how much fabric does she need in square inches? (Meyer 2012)

Now I have never made a dog bandana, and I suspect my dog wouldn't tolerate one. But if you were making one, wouldn't you make a good guess and just try it on?

Perhaps the most famous mockery of word problems occurred in the film, *How Green Was My Valley,* when Huw Morgan's father is trying to help him with an algebra problem. He begins by reading the problem:

> The bathtub holds 100 gallons. "A" fills it at the rate of 20 gallons a minute and "B" at the rate of ten gallons a minute. Got that, Mr. Morgan?
>
> Huw: Twenty and ten gallons. Yes, sir.
>
> Father: Now then. "C" is a hole that empties it at the rate of five gallons a minute. How long to fill the tub?

The problem is so nonsensical that it sends Huw's mother Beth into hysterics: "Who would pour water in a bathtub full of holes? Who would think of it? Only a madman."

Falling Off the Truck

I know I am not alone in this self-consciousness and insecurity about math. Sometimes I picture the progression of math education like riding in the back of an open, flatbed truck, say a Ford 150. Initially, the ride is relatively smooth and it is easy to hold on, but as it moves into the middle and high school years, the truck speeds up. The road becomes increasingly bumpy and rutted. And we begin to fall off. But the truck doesn't stop. It just keeps barreling along—until by the end of high school and the beginning of college, almost everyone is off the truck. They still may be taking math courses (because they are required) but they have checked out mentally. They've been convinced that math is not their thing.

According to math educator Tracy Zager, author of *Becoming the Math Teacher You Wish You'd Had* (2017), the timed testing of math facts is a prime early cause of math anxiety. "If we could eliminate that practice, we would make an enormous difference for kids. People just hate it." She also noted that for many who have fallen off the truck, the cause is a

According to math educator Tracy Zager, the timed testing of math facts is a prime early cause of math anxiety. "If we could eliminate that practice, we would make an enormous difference for kids. People just hate it."

particular incident of shaming—the quintessential moment being an adolescent girl, probably self-conscious to begin with, failing to solve a math problem at the black (or now white) board. Or it may have been the overt frustration of a tutor or teacher that the student went to for help, perhaps nothing more than a frustrated sigh. Zager, who works with elementary school teachers, many of whom never felt at home with math, claims that telling these stories, "raveling back," must be part of inservice work, a necessary part of the therapy.

Her own story, although not particularly shaming, is representative of math instruction with no place of curiosity. Her algebra class was being taught exponents, and her teacher informed the class that numbers to the first power were themselves; but all numbers to the zero power were one. All numbers. This made no sense to her. She asked, "Why wouldn't it be zero? Why would one be the starting point?" The teacher had no answer, felt his authority questioned, and finally said that's just the way it is. "He could have stopped and said, 'I don't know. That's an interesting question that we should investigate.'" But it became one of those "flashbulb memories" that colored her view of math.

The wonder is that our educational system has for decades tolerated this attrition, to the point it seems like the natural weaning of math talent. That's what happened to my wife in college in the late 1960s. She wanted to be a math major and came to Oberlin with a 770 SAT score in math, which probably put her in an elite group of women, skilled and interested in going on. But she had difficulty with calculus and was counseled out of taking more math, in her freshman year. At a time when there was a desperate need for women to enter mathematics and math education, she was collateral damage. That's just the way things are.

> In his book, *The Math Myth*, Andrew Hacker argues that one reason for the discomfort, and shame, is that we are caught in a system that requires a level and type of training in math that is difficult for those who fall off the truck, and not connected to the real needs for quantitative reasoning that jobs require.

In his book, *The Math Myth* (2016), Andrew Hacker argues that one reason for the discomfort, and shame, is that we are caught in a system that requires a level and type of training in math that is difficult for those who fall off the truck, and not connected to the real needs for quantitative reasoning that jobs require. According to an analysis by the Educational Testing Service, only 5 percent of jobs actually require advanced mathematics (Carnevale and Desrochers 2003)—courses that are typically required of all college applicants. And even that number probably overstates the case, as many of the professions in this elite 5 percent like computer programmer make little use of advanced math.

The ETS study concludes: "The mismatch between high school mathematics courses and the quantitative literacy required on the job suggests that a large share of Americans have either too much math or the wrong kind" (Carnevale and Desrochers 2003, 27). It should be noted that Hacker's book (which builds on the ETS study) is roundly detested by math educators who claim that the problems lie in instruction, and not in the demand for advanced mathematics—Hacker, in their view, is urging capitulation and defeatism. They argue that the solution is not to abandon the traditional subjects, but to make them more grounded, engaging, and possible.

Take my own case. I am chair of a school board that each year authorizes about $40 million in expenditures—we virtually set the tax rate for our district. Each meeting involves some kind of spreadsheet—on enrollment, budget, class size, teacher salary and benefits, test scores. What is required of us is a *number sense*, the capacity to see trends, surprises, problems—stories—in these numbers. We rarely make exact calculations but we estimate like crazy. For example, because the primary grade enrollments are down (as they are throughout New England), we need to be shifting teachers to higher grades to avoid layoffs. What certificates will they need to make that switch? Good board members have a feel for these numbers, an eye for the one significant number on an Excel spreadsheet.

I actually love quantification. I find it reassuring, stabilizing, rooted in my love of sports and sports statistics. I love the precision it brings to impressions or attitudes—the way a solid statistic can disrupt a story—like the one Donald Trump is now telling about the criminality of immigrants, when *in fact they are less likely to commit crimes*. We are predisposed to construct stories on the most easily accessible information, often a sensational news story, or even an image: there is a school shooting and we tell ourselves a story of the increase in school violence, the danger kids face in schools, when schools, statistically, are one of the safest places to be. Numbers make me a better citizen, and a better board member.

At an even deeper level, for me at least, numbers are a predictable system in a world that often seems unpredictable—which may be why many of those on the autism spectrum are drawn to math. We live so much of our lives in a hazy world of impressions, subjectivities, opinion, uncertainties about how to act or what is actually happening. I can easily imagine, and indeed feel, the attraction for a realm that is less hazy, less dependent on tacit and unspoken codes of behavior, and patterned.

Why We Fall Off

The problem for students—their alienation—occurs when the problem is given and not formulated by the student; it has no roots in curiosity, or even the students' reality (all those damn trains speeding toward each other). My friend Cris Tovani tells the story of checking the reasoning of some Colorado students who missed what should have been an easy problem on how much distance would have to be covered to plow a field. The calculation should have been simple. But in talking with kids she learned that the problem was that they had never seen an agricultural plow—only snowplows.

We may feel anxiety when the dial is turned to pure mathematical formulation too soon. And it occurs when the goal, always, is getting the exact right answer—when a good approximation will do. Good guessing is also a good check on how reasonable a calculation is—when it doesn't look right.

We might define shame as a disabling story we tell ourselves to account for difficulty. It is disabling (and distorting) because we put the full responsibility on ourselves. It is a personal deficiency, internalized, not the result of a system in which failure and attrition are expected outcomes. A difficulty becomes an identity; we move from "I have trouble converting fractions" to "I'm not good at math." And identities, once formed, are hard to change, even when they are not working for us.

If we were to identify the roots of math shame, invitations to believe "I am not a math person," these might be some of them:

- **Pace.** More than any other subject, math is cumulative, one concept building on another. Consequently it is easier, and dangerous, to fall behind. Thus begins a downward spiral that is hard to arrest. Typically US schools try to cover more problems in a class than their counterparts in high-performing countries like Japan—though the problems in Japan might be more difficult (Stigler and Hiebert 2009).

- **Mystification.** Just as for years writing was seen as a pure talent, with the messy process of composing obscured, I believe many students see math ability as a sort of gift. The contrast between stage and backstage is a useful metaphor. Students see the stage—the orderly and successful solving of problems, always arriving at the exact right answer. But they don't see the backstage—the false starts, puzzlement, uncertainty, playfulness of math thinking. Students hear of the "beauty" of math, the deep pleasure of mathematical work, even its comparability to music. But there is very little music in what they do.
- **Abstraction.** As students move through the grades, math seems increasingly a formal, abstract system, unrelated to their life experiences. Even the attempts to make it real, those story problems, are not rooted in any decision or question they have (like the juice mixture "problem" cited earlier). Although algebra, often basic algebra, is integrated into science classes—there is far less attention paid to the role of quantitative reasoning in civics or sociology (e.g., the capacity to analyze data sets in the US census—where Andrew Hacker is a wizard!).
- **Time.** I have already dealt with this. Particularly in testing situations, deliberateness is penalized. If we are really interested in persistence and grit, we need to allow time to stay with a problem. The standard advice on tests is, if you are having trouble and can eliminate one or two answers, guess and go on. What message does that send?
- **Helplessness.** In reading instruction one of the key concepts is "repair." If you have misread something, or experienced a difficulty, you have strategies to right yourself. I think we have all experienced helplessness with computer problems—where we have *one* strategy (which sometimes works): turn the machine off and start again. In other words, we need options to revise our thinking, and I believe this happens in the solution of math problems. It would also make more sense to have students work the same problem in multiple ways with other students than to relentlessly have to complete a problem set. This multiple solution approach is more typical of Japanese math instruction.

This feeling of helplessness is not exclusively a US problem. According to the 2012 Programme for International Student Assessment (PISA) international study, "Some 30% of students reported that they feel helpless when doing mathematics problems: 25% of boys, 35% of girls, 35% of disadvantaged students, and 24% of advantaged students reported feeling that way" (PISA 2014, 17).

The PISA highlights a major gender issue:

> Even **when girls perform as well as boys in mathematics**, they tend to report less perseverance, less openness to problem solving, less intrinsic and instrumental motivation to learn mathematics, less self-belief in their ability to learn mathematics and more anxiety about mathematics than boys, on average; they are also more likely than boys to attribute failure in mathematics to themselves rather than to external factors. (17)

- **Entrapment.** In the criminal system, entrapment is a strategy to induce someone to commit a crime. In math it looks something like this:

  > A bat and ball cost $1.10. The bat costs $1 more than the ball. How much does the ball cost?

  You can bet that one of the possible answers is $.10. It feels intuitively right. It feels attractive at first—but it is wrong (the correct answer is $.05). It could be argued that this is a good kind of problem to have us check our instinct to pick $.10. But I think problems like this one create the impression that we are always being tricked or seduced into a wrong answer. This creates what rhetoricians would call a problem with "ethos"—the test maker is hostile, cunning, trying to make us fail. In fact, the test makers need us (or some of us) to fail to produce a distribution.

- **Isolation**. Many math classes, particularly at the high school level, are built on homework, usually done in isolation, away from any more knowledgeable practitioner (parents are reluctant to help because of unfamiliar new terminology, not to mention their own math histories). Thus the great paradox of homework. If the problems involve a mastered skill, that skill may be reinforced, though too much repetition can lead to drudgery. *But* if the skill is not relatively secure, there is no timely help for the learner. In their portrait of high-performing Japanese schools, Stigler and Hiebert (2009) observed that there was more emphasis on collaborative groups of students working on a few difficult problems, often coming up with multiple solutions.

This may seem an overcritical list, but what is striking about the new generation of math reformers is the severity of their own criticism. Here is Dan Meyer:

> Please imagine a time when you really loved something—a movie, an album, a song or a book—and you recommended it wholeheartedly to someone you also really liked. And you anticipated their reaction—and they hated it. So by way of introduction, that's the same state in which I've spent every working day for the last six years. I teach high school math. I sell a product to a market that doesn't want it but is forced by law to buy it. It's just a losing proposition. (2010)

Or how about this passage on school geometry from Paul Lockhart's widely circulated jeremiad, A *Mathematician's Lament*:

> Posing as the arena in which students will finally get to engage in mathematical reasoning, this virus [i.e., school geometry] attacks mathematics at its heart, destroying the very essence of creative rational argument, poisoning the students' enjoyment of this fascinating and beautiful subject, and permanently disabling them from thinking about math in a natural and intuitive way. (2009, 67)

Take that!

The student response to these learning or testing situations is often termed "math anxiety," about which there is a huge literature. But the very term seems to put the locus of the problem on the learner and not the situation or culture of mathematics education. It is possible to feel anxiety in situations that you fully support and don't wish to change—the anxiety before a swimming meet, a musical performance. But math anxiety, it seems to me, is the near-inevitable product of a system traditionally bent on winnowing; on identifying, supporting, and advancing the most proficient students. Those who are winnowed out, programmatically or psychologically, decide they are "not good at math."

As I see it, mathematics education is caught between two opposing principles. One, as I have noted previously, is the principle of winnowing, the progressive narrowing of the pool of students who can master its abstraction and formalism, all on the inevitable march toward calculus. There is the acceptance, even expectation, that most students will fall by the wayside. Opposed but coexisting with that principle is the expectation that math is coequal to reading and writing and should be required of all students, actually the more the better, and that subjects like advanced algebra and trigonometry should be universal requirements. And often this justification is that these math proficiencies are broadly necessary for the jobs of the future—a claim that is patently false.

Put another way, which is the right Biblical parable? The story about separating the wheat from the chaff? Or the parable of the shepherd who must retrieve the one lost sheep? It is about falling off the truck—or making sure everyone stays on. Is it about the march to calculus, a winnowing of talent? Or making math a language that everyone can speak, a birthright, a democratized proficiency like reading?

Low Threshold for Entry

The term *low threshold* will take significance in the remainder of this book. A threshold is an entry point, perhaps a guess, a beginning sentence of a freewrite, an initial response to the title of a book or chapter, a feeling that I can get started on this, get some kind of toehold. Dan Meyer, for example, famously takes textbook math problems and removes all of the information that obscures the basic problem—bit by bit he performs a mathematical striptease, taking us to the core question and inviting us to speculate on an answer, to make a good guess—and only later moving to calculation and terminology (another difference between US and Japanese schools is our emphasis on terminology).

Suppose I gave you these questions: "Which of the following five numbers doesn't belong? And why do you think it doesn't belong?" No terms, definitions in advance—just the questions—and the assurance that there is no one right answer.

5, 10, 15, 20, 25

- You could make a case for 5, because we can only get it by multiplying it by 1—all the others can be created by other combinations, in addition to 1.
- You could make a case for 25—the only number created by multiplying a number by itself.
- You could make a case for 20—which can be made by multiplying three numbers together (2 × 5 × 2). It's the only one that can be done that way.
- You could make a case for 15—it is the only number that could be created by multiplying by 3.

I was initially stumped by the 10, but you could say it is the only number that is half of one number on the list and double of another.

Even in this short exercise we have touched on some key features of math—factors (a number or quantity that when multiplied with another produces a given number or expression); prime numbers (those that cannot be factored); squares (those multiplied by themselves). But rather than proceeding deductively with definitions first, we proceed more simply through our questions, observations, intuitions about the numbers (and it would be nice to have an abundance of blocks around to play with combinations). We have an easy entry point or threshold.

A masterful example of the low threshold approach to math thinking is Christopher Danielson's disarmingly wonderful book *Which One Doesn't Belong?* (2016). It begins with this simple invitation: "This book is different from other books about shapes. Every page asks the same question, and every answer can be correct. Turn the page and see for yourself." We see four shapes and are asked, "Which one doesn't belong?" (Figure 6-1).

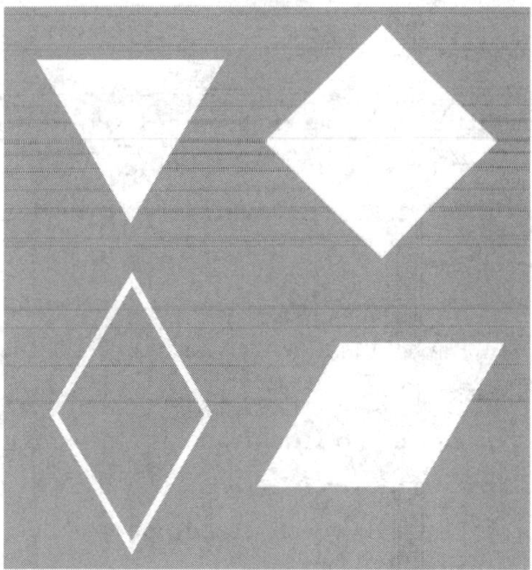

Figure 6-1

Is it the three-sided figure, or the one with every corner equal? (But are there two like that?) The one with the uncolored interior? Without formal naming, we play with concepts—perimeter, area, angles (acute, right, obtuse), shapes (parallelogram, square, triangle, diamond). But this language isn't imposed: we are invited to use our own language. The parallelogram is "leaning over." Or maybe it's the only one that isn't balanced on a point—your call. The key is coming up with a justification.

As I worked through some of Danielson's pages, I was reminded of Jean Jacque-Rousseau's great insights into math. Rousseau scorned teaching practices that substituted words for things—and held up prodigies as examples of miseducation: they know the words but don't have real understanding that can only come through manipulation of *things*. For Danielson, the key is not having the right word, but finding one's own language to describe differences.

I decided to play with the "Which One Doesn't Belong?" idea with various containers in our kitchen (Figure 6-2).

Would it be the coffee cup, with its constant width? The wine glass with its curved shape? The dark coffee mug could be chosen because it seems to have two sections similar to the coffee cup. The wine bottle seems a combination of uniform sections (the neck and main part of the bottle) and two curving sections (underneath and connecting the main part of the bottle and the neck).

Figure 6-2

But as I looked at the picture, I asked a different question that I think Danielson would approve of: how are all these the same? They are all circular, right? Which leads to the question: what is it about circles that makes them the preferred container for fluids? Why don't we drink out of square cups?

Maybe it has to do with pouring (or cleaning). But it also may be efficiency. That would make sense—to economize on materials you want to have the most interior space with the least container surface. All of which made me think of blowing bubbles—which naturally take the form of spheres. Sometimes, if you blow slightly too hard, they form oblongs, which either right themselves to a sphere—or pop. Could it be that the soap material "finds" its way to the most stable shape, which would be the shape with the least surface area for the volume?

I raised this question of insides and outsides with Tracy Zager, and she immediately linked to biological survival:

> So much of biology is about this issue of insides and outsides. For example, a friend of mine who is a wildlife biologist was studying the shape of protected lands and invasive species. The more circular, the better. Why? Because a circle has the least outside relative to its inside. It's the same reason why the cross section of a tree is a circle. Bark is protective and takes energy to create. The tree wants to make as little of it as possible while maintaining its protection.

I'm thinking—wow, have we connected wine bottles, soap bubbles, and tree bark. All three have something to do with the efficiency of circles.

But back to my which-one-is-different task. Could I find containers that really would be different from the four that I picked? And you can see them in Figure 6-3: I found them.

Figure 6-3

If the most efficient container, meaning the least surface for volume, is circular—why have the makers of these products chosen the less efficient form? The answer seems obvious—packing. I learned that packing of spheres has long been a major mathematical challenge; the great German mathematician Carl Gauss is credited with determining the maximum density for packing spheres (historically a concern for storing cannonballs). Spherical bottles would lose space in a box, while the square base allows for tighter packing. The trade-off may be between material cost on one hand and shipping/storing/shelf space costs—which I imagine is a major calculation for those who design containers and packages.

Is This What Real Math Feels Like?

Near the end of my interview with Tracy Zager, she brought up the topic of interesting mistakes and, as an example, showed me this one. A student had converted the multiplication problem:

$$38 \times 22$$

to:

$$40 \times 20 = 400$$

The answer is wrong, but the student has taken a useful rule from addition and applied it to multiplication. If we were adding 38 + 22 it would equal 40 + 20. So

Tracy's question to me was: why does this process work in adding but not in multiplying?

I'm ashamed to say that my initial response was "because multiplication is different from addition"—but of course that is simply circular. It's different because it is different. That would be about as helpful as Zager's teacher saying 4 to the 0 power is 1—and that's just the way it is.

As I drove home, and all that evening, I obsessed about her question. I should be able to do better than give a circular answer. In my admittedly sketchy reading of math educators, I noticed that they tended to draw math problems as shapes and figures—to visualize them—and I decided to give it a try.

First, I simplified the problem: 2 × 6 does not equal 4 × 4.

And I drew them as seen in Figure 6-4.

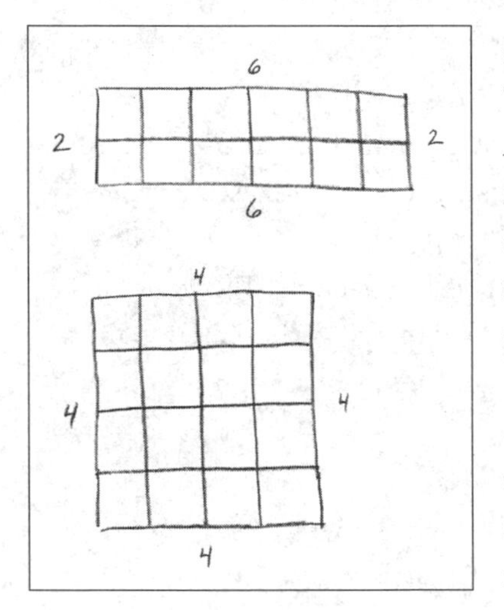

Figure 6-4

As I did that it became clear that *every multiplication problem created a rectangle.* That had never occurred to me before. Addition seemed to me more like walking along a line—if I took two steps, paused and took six more steps—I would end up in the same place as if I taken two stages of four steps.

But rectangles were different. In *A Mathematician's Lament*, Paul Lockhart (2009) suggests that we observe the "behavior" of shapes and numbers, as if we were studying hamsters. So what do we notice about rectangles that have borders or perimeters of the same length? Imagine that I am walking around these two rectangles (4 × 4 and 6 × 2)—I would walk the same distance. But the square is more efficient at holding stuff, more area.

Could we predict, then, that if you hold the sum of the two multiplied numbers equal, the closer they are to each other, the higher the multiplied result? Could we make that rule, define that pattern, identify that "behavior"? Can we say that the closer they are to forming a square, the bigger the multiplied result? Let's try.

Because 38 × 22 is more squarish than 40 × 20, it should be the higher number—and it is, 836 to 800.

Put another way, the square seems more efficient at holding area than a rectangle with different lengths and heights. All of which called to mind images of flying over the heartland of the United States—the seemingly endless square miles of cultivated land that creates such a tapestry. If you are fencing in land, it makes sense to get the most enclosure for the least fence, and the square is the most efficient rectangle for doing that.

So is this the kind of exploration that Lockhart and some of the other math reformers are talking about? It feels right, open in a way that my math courses never were, directed by my own curiosity. He ends by offering us this "practical" advice:

> Just play! You don't need a license to do math. You don't need to take a class or read a book. Mathematical Reality is *yours* to enjoy for the rest of your life. It exists in your imagination and you can do whatever you want with it. (2009, 139)

For a fleeting moment, I felt close to this Mathematical Reality.

49 + (18 – 3) = 64

After the sinking of the Titanic, a lifeboat with a strict capacity for 64 people was nearly full with 49 rescued passengers. Those on the boat could see 18 struggling passengers in the water—they counted again and yet again it came to 18. They would be able to pick up 15 of them, but 3 would have to be left in the freezing water to die of hypothermia. One by one they picked up those who seemed younger, or middle aged, leaving an older couple and an aged man clinging to a wooden door floating in the water. As the boat turned away from these 3, the older passengers called for help but the boat left the area, because those in the boat could not stand hearing the cries.

The Rope

A new generation of math educators recognizes the attitudinal barriers they face—and seeks to democratize it, make it a language for all, recover a sense of wonder. One undoubtedly positive development in math education is the proliferation of clubs and extracurricular contests that push students to use their math knowledge in creative ways, often embedded in stories or scenarios. In an *Atlantic Monthly* article, Peg Tyre describes how children at one "Russian School" (an after-school math program that enrolls 17,500 students nationwide) asked students to explain the expression 49 + (18 – 3) in a narrative. Students "invented stories of fruit, the shedding and growing of teeth, and to the amusement of all, toilet monsters" (Tyre 2016). See my effort in the box on page 117.

The focus on these schools is on problem-solving, applying knowledge to "open ended, multi-faceted situations that can be solved by using different approaches." Take, for example, one scenario from the expii.com website developed by Po-Shen Loh, math professor at Carnegie Mellon University:

> Imagine a rope that runs completely around the Earth's equator, flat against the ground (assume the Earth is a perfect sphere, without any mountains or valleys). You cut the rope and tie in another piece of rope that is 710 inches long, or just under 60 feet. That increases the total length of the rope by a bit more than the length of a bus, or the height of a 5-story building. Now imagine that the rope is lifted at all points simultaneously, so that it floats above the Earth at the same height all along its length. What is the largest thing that could fit underneath the rope? (in Tyre 2016).

The options are: bacteria, a lady bug, a dog, Einstein, a giraffe, or a space shuttle.

This is such an arresting image—a rope around the entire world, with an extra section, that is lifted uniformly. My first reaction (and that of almost everyone to whom I have presented this problem) is that, given the immense size of the earth a piddly 60 feet will make almost no difference—even the bacteria would have to bend over. And I am sure I will need to know the circumference of the Earth, but it is not given, so I will have to make do without it. I dredge up the geometry facts I know. And I conclude that what I need to figure out is the change in the *radius* when the *circumference* of the Earth expands by 60 feet. And as I recall there is a fixed formula for the relationship—I look it up: circumference = $\pi \times$ diameter.

Because it takes two radii to make a diameter, I have this to work with:

$$\text{Circumference} = \pi \times 2r$$

Substitute the numbers:

$$60 = 3.14 \times 2r$$

Divide both sides by 2:

$$30 = 3.14\, r$$

Divide both sides by 3.14:

$$r = 9.54$$

(The answer is Einstein, with a few feet to spare.)

I feel very proud and show this to my wife, who is way better than I am at math. She asks, "So you assume (bit of sarcasm) that you don't need to know the size of the circle. How could you prove that?"

I realize what I am saying is that *any* circle with the circumference increased by 60 feet would have a radius increase of 9.54 feet. So what if we had a small circle with a circumference of 10 feet (a big beach ball) and added that extra 60 feet?

I run through the same steps and come to an answer of 9.56 feet, which I will call identical with the rounding I did. *It doesn't matter the size of the circle.* Einstein could stand under the rope here too, though he might have trouble balancing on a beach ball. He would fit under any rope expanded 60 feet, around any sphere, Jupiter, the entire solar system if we could imagine it as a sphere.

How can I explain the difference between this real problem and the abstract one that I started this chapter with? It is, I think, the engaging narrative situation that frames the math. The image of the lifting rope, and determining the space beneath it. I felt motivated, captivated, by the problem of space that was created, the impossibility of not making a prediction. It is also the confounding of my expectation that this space beneath the rope would be infinitesimal. It gave me the gratifying feeling that I had the tools, the formula and concepts (radius, circumference, pi), to do the work. And it gave me a momentary glimpse of what mathematicians call beauty, the uniform relationships between radius and circumference, which, because of this one problem, is vividly in my consciousness. The wonder of pi.

I dream of that rope.

CHAPTER 7

Reading Guilt

The Art and Science of Forgetting

Without forgetting, it is quite impossible to live at all.

—**FRIEDRICH NIETZSCHE**, *ON THE ADVANTAGES AND DISADVANTAGES OF HISTORY FOR LIFE*

The term *comprehension* is derived from the Latin word for holding or grasping—and that makes sense. If we did not hold onto facts, images, and propositions in our reading, what would be the point? If we did not retain information in informational texts, why would we ever bother to read them? But comprehension is even more the act of forgetting, or selectively forgetting, or radically reducing what we have read to a "gist." It is more about letting go than about holding on.

You are doing that now. You are (I hope) "comprehending" every word I have written so far, but transforming or reducing this opening into something very compact (Newkirk, reading, forgetting). If it stays with you at all, if it finds a precious place in your long-term memory, it will exist as a compact proposition with perhaps a few anchoring details (and even this retained bit is unstable). That is all I can hope for. This chapter on forgetting will be mostly forgotten.

And that is as it should be.

The classic description case of a perfect memory for detail is Aleksandr Luria's (1968) brilliant case study of S., a Russian journalist, whom he interviewed and examined over a thirty-year period. S. could easily take into memory a chart of sixty random numbers—and recall them decades later. His technique was to create images or even personalities for each of the numbers: 87, for example, was a fat woman accompanied by a man twirling his moustache. He would create a story in which, on an imaginary walk, he would encounter images for each of the words or numbers to be recalled. But what S. could not do is generalize or grasp the meaning of something he read: it was as if the images closed off any possibility of stepping back and interpreting. He could not let go of the elaborate detail—he couldn't forget. And, in the end, this was a major disability for him.

His case dramatically illustrates the cognitive necessity of forgetting, at least forgetting detail. Memory, of course, defines us as human, as a self, and when we cease to remember we lose our identity. But to operate we must have ways of ignoring most detail—selecting, condensing, distilling, and abstracting. If we couldn't economize in this way, we would overload our memory. In the rest of this chapter I want to speculate on what we can reasonably comprehend, hold on to, and what we must necessarily let go of—or simply fail to attend to in the first place.

This short foray in forgetting is fitting for a book on embarrassment because memory seems, for so many of us, so often, such an unreliable faculty. We need to prop it up with reminders, calendars, alerts—and, if you're like me, you have to remember to check the reminder. We collect physical "souvenirs" to recapture our past. More significantly, there is the haunting sense that so much of our lives, including what we read, slips into oblivion, never to be recovered. Entire years seem to vanish. Or we can barely recall a few key details from a book we know we liked reading. We're stunned by these lapses and think—I should be better at this.

There are to be sure other forms of embarrassment connected to reading—particularly oral reading, as we have already seen with Aeriale in the chapter on stigma (and who can forget the pain of the stumbling oral reading of Shakespeare?). David Pillemer and his colleagues who have collected key episodic memories of English classes note that shame often occurs when students are told that an interpretation they make of a text is wrong. Here is one such memory:

> In my sophomore year, I took an English literature course. I loved the course material, enjoyed writing papers, and felt pretty good about them until . . . I wrote an essay on my interpretation of a poem. I felt I had great insight into a special meaning within a verse. When the paper was returned, the teacher told me I didn't have any understanding of the material and she hoped I wasn't going to be an English major. I

> remember her pinched face and small, tight mouth as she said these things to me. I thought no way do I want to be like her. So I changed my major from English to Sociology. (Pillemer et al. 1996, 333)

These are all trails this chapter could take. But I will focus on something less traumatic and more a regular human failing: the ways that our fallible and forgetful readings fall short of an ideal—an inhuman form of attentiveness and retention, a capacity to grasp and hold. So much slips though the fingers of our memory.

Saliency

Imagine that in your reading of a text you retained a blurry map written on onionskin paper, super thin and fragile, a slight breeze will send it moving. But it is held in place by a few pins—and those pins are salient facts, or episodes, or images. Museum specialists call this "sticky" information. Here is an example: In a conversation with my father, I told him I was finally reading Rousseau's *Confessions,* which I knew he had read because I had seen the book around the house. He asked, "Did you get to the part about the shirts?"

"No," I said, "what's that about?"

"Well, you know how Rousseau is always complaining about lack of recognition and money. Then he has thirty-seven shirts stolen. How poor could he have been?"

I asked him how long since he had read the book. "Just after the war, I think." In other words, forty years earlier. This fact, the stolen shirts, is an anchoring detail that he holds in place, like a pin, an impression of Rousseau as not wholly truthful—and a bit of a whiner.

I can think of numerous other examples. I loved reading Stephen Ambrose's *Undaunted Courage* (1997), the moving account of the Lewis and Clark expedition. One fact that stands out for me, one of the few I retain, is that over the two years and four months of the journey, only one man among the thirty-three who set out died, because of a disease incurable at the time. This fact anchors an interpretation or inference: that Lewis and Clark were extraordinary and resourceful leaders. (And in the interests of honesty I had to look up the length of the journey and number of people in his party.)

The saliency of information is dependent on what rhetorician James Kinneavy calls "surprise value." He notes that "'information' is news, and news is the unpredictable, the unforeseen, the improbable" (1971, 93). Our brains are attuned to deviations from the normal and expected. Take this short description of female attendants on China's new high-speed trains:

> The guests are ushered aboard by female attendants in Pan Am style pill-box hats; each attendant, according to regulations, had to be at least five feet tall, and was trained to smile with exactly eight teeth visible. (Osnos 2012)

The requirement to be five feet tall is completely expected, and forgettable. But "eight teeth visible"—that is unexpected (who does the counting?). It is also an uncomfortable fact because it objectifies these women, recalling the inspection of horses. It holds our attention and stands a chance of taking space in long-term memory as an anchoring detail, or a pin that allows us to hold an impression of how meticulous, even obsessive, Chinese planners are.

To pick another example, Malcolm Gladwell (2008) begins his book *Outliers* with an analysis of the birth dates of an elite junior Canadian hockey team. Seemingly in defiance of all probability, almost all of the players on the team were born in the first six months of the year. How could it be that a December baby would have so little chance of making the team? How could birth dates have such an impact on selection that we presume is based on merit? Gladwell shows that it goes back to earlier selections for youth teams where a January birth would have almost a whole year development edge over the December birth—this could be a big deal when you are talking about five-year-olds. His point is that luck plays a big role in opportunity and success—and he makes the point with an unforgettable case.

Not only is this Gladwell story surprising—it is consequential, another key feature of memorable stories. As we read it we instinctively think of our own experiences, or our children's on youth teams, and recognize a hidden inequity built into seemingly benign and neutral rules.

Gladwell's exemplary stories are retained because they function as episodic memories, a term usually used to describe how we recall significant incidents in our lives (Pillemer 2001; Pillemer et al. 2015). For example, we tend to have vivid memories of originating events: first kiss, first child, first semester at college. When we toast or eulogize, we make use of these episodes ("Remember the time when . . ."). We also remember national tragedies as vivid episodes, often recalling where we were when we took in the news. Clearly we can use this form of memory for vicarious or rendered experience as well, for example, Gladwell's harrowing account of miscommunications between pilots and air traffic controllers that have resulted in catastrophic crashes.

Most texts provide multiple ways of creating these pins of selective memory—based on our prior experience, prior knowledge, purposes for reading. Each of us holds down the reading in different ways, because we pay attention in different ways. One example I use in class frequently is the opening to *A Visit from the Goon Squad* (2011) by Jennifer Egan. I ask students to read it a couple of times and mark what struck them as significant:

> It began the usual way, in the bathroom of the Lassimo Hotel. Sasha was adjusting her yellow eye shadow in the mirror when she noticed a bag on the floor beside the sink that must have belonged to the woman whose peeing she could faintly hear through the vaultlike door of the toilet stall. Inside the rim of the bag, barely visible, was a wallet made of pale green leather. It was easy for Sasha to recognize, looking back, that the peeing woman's blind trust had provoked her: *We live in a city where people will steal the hair off your head if you give them half a chance, but you leave your stuff lying in plain sight and expect it to be waiting for you when you get back?* It made her want to teach the woman a lesson. But this wish only camouflaged the deeper feeling Sasha always had: that fat, tender wallet, offering itself to her hand—it seemed so dull, so life-as-usual to just leave it there than seize the moment, accept the challenge, take the leap, fly the coop, throw caution to the wind, live dangerously ("I get it," Coz, her therapist said), and *take* the fucking thing.
>
> "You mean steal it." (2011, 3–4)

What struck *me* was Sasha's shifting rationales for taking the wallet. Was she doing it to be adventurous, to be unconventional and free, to teach a lesson? And does the fact she is talking to a psychiatrist mean she is at some level aware that these are not satisfactory explanations?

I *totally* ignored the description of Sasha putting on "yellow eye shadow." One female student asked, "What kind of woman uses yellow eye shadow? It doesn't make you look good." Another followed up, "And she seems familiar with hotel bathrooms. You know I think she's a prostitute." As it turns out this is an amazingly good prediction, but one that never could have occurred to me because I had never registered the eye shadow as "surprising." This is, of course,

Psychology 101—I lacked a schema for eye shadow. The Roman essayist Seneca claimed these differences in what we attend to were inevitable:

> There is nothing particularly surprising about this way which everyone has of deriving material for their own individual interests from identical subject matter. In one and the same meadow the cow looks for grass, the dog for the hare, and the stork for the lizard. (2004, 108)

Yet our standardized tests continue to treat the "main idea" as something *in the text,* as definite as the bone in a chicken leg.

So powerful is our attraction to these details that psychologists have coined the term *seductive details* to refer to images, facts, details so compelling that we remember them, but not the larger points or ideas that they anchor (Harp and Mayer 1998). The classic example is an advertisement that began running in 1984. Claire Peller, a diminutive eighty-two-year-old actress, examined some fast food hamburgers and asked in outrage, "Where's the beef?" Anyone from that era remembers this tagline—Walter Mondale even used the line to criticize his Democratic opponent Gary Hart. But what we don't remember is the fast food chain that *ran* the ad. I was clueless on this; my wife guessed Burger King. It was Wendy's (mocking the thin McDonald's hamburger). In other words, unless the episodes or salient details link to broader meanings, they may not serve the writer's global intentions.

There are, I believe, several implications for this inevitable, radical selectivity in our attention to written texts:

- Standardized tests predetermine salient information, and this predetermination may not correspond to a reader's pattern of attention. Hence the advice to read the questions first—hardly an ecologically valid reading experience. There can be few more unpleasant (and unrealistic) experiences than reading—with no purpose—a complex passage on a topic of no interest, and having to guess what someone else finds significant.
- Readers who feel guilty for forgetting detail in their reading (and who doesn't?) can take some comfort that this reduction frees our brain to take in larger meanings.
- A crucial skill for writers is to include "sticky" details that surprise or delight—that constitute what Kinneavy (1971) calls "information." This skill is as important for the non-fiction writer as for the writer of fiction and poetry. To

remember something it must be memorable. Steven Pinker (2014) reminds us that a good portion of our brain is given over to vision—and writers who help us visualize are more likely to anchor information in our memory.

- A narrative structure—in all genres of discourse—can promote more effective anchoring because we identify and empathize with characters. This is why widely read nonfiction writers employ narrative so deftly (Newkirk 2014).
- Any attempt to claim that initial reading of a text should stay within the "text itself" and avoid personal associations (Coleman and Pimentel 2012) is fundamentally misguided—because it is the emotional connection that enables us to attend to details in the first place. As psychologist Edmund Bolles puts it: "the emotionless observer also has a poor memory" (1988, 48).

Thematic and Emotional Memory

If we accept the fact that this forgetfulness is inevitable and that it is not caused by a lack of attentiveness, or willpower, or virtue on our part, we arrive at a conundrum, particularly in reference to informational texts. Why would we read biographies, essays, histories, if we retain so little? Isn't this the height of inefficiency and futility? Take for example my reading of Siddhartha Mukherjee's *The Emperor of All Maladies* (2011), a prize-winning account of the evolution of cancer treatment and research. My wife and I both read it at a time when she was being treated for endometrial cancer, and I found it a powerful and important book.

But what information do I recall three years later? I imagine a basic quiz that someone might give me—nothing tricky, just some foundational facts. So here were the questions on my sixty-point pop quiz:

1. Name five major researchers who made advances in the understanding and treatment of cancer. (20 points)
2. Why was childhood leukemia a good choice for early research in cancer treatment? (10 points)
3. A major breakthrough in cancer research came when cancer could be studied on the cellular level. Describe one technique used to conduct this type of study. (10 points)
4. Define *angiogenesis*. (10 points)

My score—19. And that includes giving myself full credit for putting down Dana Farber instead of Sidney Farber—the only name I recall from the entire book.

Paradoxically, I believe that we don't read extended informational texts for information. Or at least not information as we usually conceive it.

We can conclude one of two things from this performance. I was a failure because I gained very little in the way of information from the reading—less than an entry in a junior encyclopedia, which would also be more accurate. Or, what I gained from the reading was *not* information, but something else, something more akin to what we get when we read fiction. Paradoxically, I believe that we don't read extended informational texts for information. Or at least not information as we usually conceive it.

Now suppose some Lucifer-like character tempted me with this bargain. He might say something like this: "Tom, you spent how many hours reading this book, fifteen? What if I could provide a list of the information you would remember, or need to remember, and you could memorize it in just an hour? We could quiz and requiz until you had it. Then you could go back to watching those boring stages of the Tour de France that you seem to like. But the *result* would be the same. Listen, listen, I am *giving* you back those fourteen hours." I instinctively would not take this bargain because I don't believe the result would be the same.

We remember emotional states as well as factual detail and propositions—in fact, from an evolutionary standpoint this form of memory is seen as primary (Bolles 1988, 29–41). The human brain and nervous system evolved over millennia in situations where instantaneous fight-or-flight decisions were crucial, when it was necessary to determine if a situation was safe or unsafe. To wait out a long logical analysis would be dangerous and slow—better an instantaneous emotional and physical connection to previous situations. Pillemer notes that the strong involuntary emotional memories have adaptive value, rooted in our evolutionary history:

> In a world of limited environmental variation and clearly specified threats, automatic emotional and behavioral responsiveness to potentially dangerous situations would enhance the chances of survival. (1998, 174)

The dominance of emotional memory is also evident in cases of trauma where the primary and initial response is emotional, and often only by laborious analysis is the literal event, the cause of the trauma, recalled. Even with animals, my dog for example, his assessment of any situation is rooted in a bodily sense of safety or danger (the dishwasher has long been a threat).

Or take my memory of my father-in-law, now deceased. He was a gregarious member of the Greatest Generation, who returned from the Pacific and raised a family in the patriarchal style very common in the postwar period. He could strike up a conversation with anyone, and before you knew it they would be exchanging phone numbers and extending invitations to visit.

But I must admit that my primary memory of him is the emotional sense I had of being with him, an awkwardness that never vanished. As a college professor, I was in a different world that he did not understand and was not curious about. Never a question about what I was working on, so I often felt like an appendage at family gatherings.

Now as tragedies go, this is not a big one, more a missed opportunity, maybe on both our parts. But my point is about memory—what I retain from my experience with him is primarily a feeling recalled. Even now, years after his death, I can revisit that gut impression of being in a room alone with him—and we had nothing to talk about. It makes sense that memories of a feeling state should be primary, whether situations make you feel safe or threatened.

I have found few accounts of readers willing to describe their own patterns of forgetfulness. Literary critic Sven Birkerts is an exception, and his own pattern of retention gives primacy to the feeling state we retain after reading:

> If anything has changed about my reading over the years, it is that I value the state a book puts me in more than I value the specific contents. Indeed, I often find that a novel, even a well-written and compelling novel, can become a blur to me soon after I've finished it. I recollect perfectly the feeling of reading it, the mood I occupied, but I am less sure about the narrative details. It's almost as if the book were, as Wittgenstein said of his propositions, a ladder to be climbed and then discarded as it served its purpose. (1994, 84)

This description rings true for me. If I take perhaps my most favorite novel, *The Brothers Karamazov,* I recall that there is a murder at the heart of it, that the brothers are very different, and that somewhere in the book there is the famous Grand

Inquisitor section. That's about it. But I retain the feeling of reading (and rereading it), the way the talk seems to roll on and on, the feeling of being caught up in this passionate and wildly dysfunctional family, the expansive sense of the novel itself. Just to write this makes it seem like poor payment for reading an 800-page book, but it's not. That sensation of reading it, being carried away by it, is the precious gift I retain.

It might be argued that Birkerts is talking about fiction, and we do not enter a novel with the expectation of carrying away information. But for me the process is virtually the same when I read a nonfiction narrative, even a more expository book like Gladwell's *Outliers* (2008) or Michael Pollan's *In Defense of Food* (2008). After all it is the same memory capacity I am using.

Both books unfold as stories or series of stories—I am drawn to the narration, the teller. I love Pollan's capacity to be a smart-ass, as when he reminds us that even though "fat" was for a long time considered a *bad* nutrient, our brains are made up of mostly (60 percent) fat tissues, which sheath the neurons. Take that! And I still remember the sense of intimacy I felt when I read the grand opening to his book:

> Eat food. Not too much. Mostly plants.
>
> That, more or less, is the short answer to the supposedly incredibly complicated and confusing question of what we humans should eat in order to be maximally healthy.
>
> I hate to give the game away right here at the beginning of a whole book devoted to the subject, and I'm tempted to complicate matters in the interest of keeping things going for a couple hundred pages or so. I'll try to resist, but will go ahead and add a few more details to flesh out the recommendations. Like eating a little meat is not going to kill you, though it might better be approached as a side dish than a main. (Pollan 2008, 1)

Although I remember some key facts from this book (probably a page-worth again), what I really recall is being with Pollan. His irreverence, and humor. Reading, it seems to me, is a lot like friendship—what we recall is the sense we had of being with that friend, not all the specifics.

All writing—all writing—is narrated. We do not confront reality (whatever that is) directly. It is mediated by a writer, a teller, and the sensibility, humor, energy, patterns of attention of the writer help create that feeling state we retain. There is a *feel* of a Michael Pollan book, or a Doris Kearns Goodwin book, or an

All writing—all writing—is narrated. We do not confront reality (whatever that is) directly. It is mediated by a writer, a teller, and the sensibility, humor, energy, patterns of attention of the writer help create that feeling state we retain.

Elizabeth Kolbert book—and we want to be in that presence.

The principle of identification relates to what I am calling the *feeling state*. Imagine a young student, say in middle school, and a dynamic physics professor visits his class to do a demonstration on combustion. There are sparks and colors (i.e., memorable images) all designed to demonstrate the scientific principle of kindling point. But what that student may retain from that demonstration may be a feeling state, a sense of attraction, a desire to one day "be like" that physics professor. That feeling of identification, of attraction, may overpower, outlast, and be more significant—than the actual lesson.

I think the same holds true in reading. For me the great model of reading was my father, a biology professor who read all the great books, or at least that is the way it seemed to me at the time. Many of the books in our house were Modern Library classics, with winged Mercury on the spine, which my mother sent to him during the war. Some would have inscriptions at the back: "New Guinea, 1944" or "Philippines, 1945." I would come home from elementary school and he would be pacing the floor reading his favorites, and none was more favorite than Montaigne.

It would be years until I read Montaigne and I could see why my dad loved him, and I came to love him too—not for any propositional learning—but for the man, for the pleasure of being in his presence, in gratitude for the kind of writing he created, the essay, the very form I am writing in now. As I read him I wanted to be like him, open like him, skeptical like him, widely read like him. I wanted to be concrete and grounded like him—as Emerson said of Montaigne: "Cut these words and they would bleed: they are vascular and alive" (2003, 325).

When we read nonfiction, we clearly retain more than this feeling state, more than the sensation of the reading. What we do retain, though, beyond salient details, and feeling states, is condensed into a theme, or narrative arc, or what psychologists call a "gist." To take *The Emperor of All Maladies* (Mukherjee 2011) as an example, I believe that what I retain is a sense of the difficulty of cancer research, a pattern of hope and disappointment, and the unbelievable heroism of doctors, researchers, and patients, many of whom went through grueling experimental trials that would help later patients. I retain a sense of the intricacy of cell division and how it is controlled and not controlled. Cancer, itself, seemed to me a character in the book, evasive, adaptable, multiple—Mukherjee even subtitles his book "A Biography of Cancer." Although the details of the book, as evidenced by my quiz, are mostly gone, the broad narrative lines of the book stay with me as a quest plot.

If I am right about the centrality of the feeling state in our recollection of reading experiences, that may seem embarrassing. There is long tradition that connects feeling and emotionality to women. *Sentimental* is about the worst thing you can call an academic. Feminist scholars have fought back with their valorization of embodied knowing and an ethic of care.

But why should we feel embarrassed by our own nature? By the ways our memories actually work? Why should we run from ourselves? Montaigne (1987) had a few words to say about this in his great concluding essay, "On Experience," criticizing those who sought to "escape from their humanity":

> We seek other attributes because we do not understand the use of our own; and having no knowledge of what is within, we sally forth outside ourselves. A fine thing to get up on stilts: for even on stilts we must ever walk with our legs. (1987, 1268–1269)

We attempt these futile "escapes" to deny the emotional grounding for our readings and our thoughts.

So, to resolve the mystery of why I would reject the Luciferian bargain of the list of facts—and break the unbearable suspense—I believe that the facts I do retain from *The Emperor of All Maladies* have an emotional grounding. Even if I could possess the facts, for example, of the use of radical mastectomies in the mid 1900s, that possession of fact is not anchored in the feeling state I experienced when reading about it, the sense of disfigurement and arrogance on the part of those who insisted that the deeper they went, the more of the pectoral and shoulder muscles they cut out, the better. There is some aura around the facts I retain; they connect to an experience of reading; they are alive.

* * * *

Few of our capacities cause us as much anxiety as memory. We feel a shiver when a familiar name escapes us. We all live in fear of dementia and can take our forgetfulness ("Where did I park that car?") as sign that we are on our way. There is the gnawing sense that if we paid more attention, focused, took notes, underlined, took courses—whatever—we would be better at retaining what we read. We can be appalled that, given the richness of our moment-by-moment activity, we retain so little—that we could read an entire book, filled with information, and could not retain more than a solid single notebook page.

Even Plato expressed anxiety about reading and memory in his dialogue *The Phaedrus* (1990). He relates the mythological story of the creation of writing by the god Theuth, who presented his invention to Thamus, king of all Egypt, claiming it will make Egyptians wiser and improve their memories. Thamus rejects this claim: "For this invention will produce forgetfulness in the minds of those who learn to use it, because they will not practice their memory" (140). Theuth has "invented an elixir not of memory, but of reminding" (140). In other words, with information recorded externally, in written language, we will not have to take information in, possess it internally—and our memory capacity will wither.

Plato was wrong, of course. The fact that this quote has stayed with me—since I read it in the University of Texas library in 1977—is a point of proof against his assertion. Memory is active in reading, but limited and reductive, necessarily so. As readers and writers we welcome the "reminding function" of writing, particularly now with the Internet making available any fact we could desire without the need of holding it in memory. This externalization of memory is a huge asset—but prior knowledge is the best determiner of reading success, and we need that knowledge instantly available.

But with the reading of longer texts, fiction and nonfiction, we have evolved economical ways of grasping what we read, economical because we can selectively and strategically forget. I have argued that we execute this strategy by enacting three forms of reduction:

Salient—focusing on a limited number of details, facts, images, episodes that help pin down our reaction to the reading. This is "sticky" information, surprising, dramatic, or directly related to personal interest.

Emotional—our retention of reading is not exclusively, or even primarily, conceptual. We retain a feeling state with books, just as we do with people.

We recall the sensation of being with them, with authors, narrators, characters. Our loyalty to authors is due, I believe, to their ability to place us in this feeling state, what Nancie Atwell calls "the reading zone" (2007).

Thematic—we retain the gist, or narrative arch, or broad theme of what we read. This theme is anchored or as I have described, pinned down by the salient details or remembered episodes the author provides.

These forms of retention allow us to forget, or even fail to register, much of what we read and experience—ultimately a great gift.

To return to *The Emperor of All Maladies,* I showed my wife my failing quiz, and it occurred to me that I had never asked her directly what the book meant to her. I still recall her reading it, bald from chemo with that telltale red scarf. In response she wrote this summation:

> It was a deeply personal read for me as I tried to make sense of my cancer diagnosis. I can recall few facts, but the reading itself calmed me as I connected what I read to my own story. Two big concepts have stayed with me. I didn't really understand the cell chemistry, but I came to see why cancer is considered a condition rather than an illness. We don't cure cancer, we *manage* it. We react to cell mutation. I also learned from people whose names and individual stories have blurred in my mind. The cumulative effect of reading all the stories of cancer patients was the realization that a cancer diagnosis takes one on a journey. You just keep moving forward until there is no place to go. That's what people have always done, and that's what those brave individuals I meet at the Cancer Center continue to do.

I'd call this comprehension.

(CHAPTER 8)

Telling a Better Story About Writing

"It's dirty to keep yelling 'digression' . . ."

—J. D. SALINGER, *CATCHER IN THE RYE*

As a writing teacher, it pains me to admit to the close association of writing and shame. But it is there. Writing is far more exposing and embarrassing—potentially—than reading, though it is not hard to find stories about the humiliation of oral reading. Classroom studies show that lower-track students do a lot more oral reading, creating vulnerability and exposure (Walmsley and Allington 1995, 26). And it could be argued that reading is conventionally equated with basic intelligence. There is even a Roman insult—"He can't read or swim"—that is, he is a loser because he hasn't mastered these normal skills.

Silent reading, though, is hidden. I misread a word, and . . . who knows. But writing is public, and often *no tolerance*. A friend of mine tells the story of how her mother, when being courted by the man who would become her husband, almost didn't respond to his letter because she was embarrassed by her handwriting. There is also a tradition of marking up papers that can only be seen as shame inducing. In Figure 8-1 you can see a model of theme correcting from Harvard, circa 1900.

Bear in mind that this is a model of effective responding.

One can only envision this reader, if we can even use that word, as hostile, superior, entitled to throw out negative comments like "vague" and "choppy" along with enigmatic question marks and directives, alluding to unstated grammatical rules. The student's page is literally disfigured. Even worse are gratuitous sarcastic comments or those accusing writers of plagiarism ("This is *not* your word!") that can haunt for a lifetime. Such alas in the heritage of composition marking.

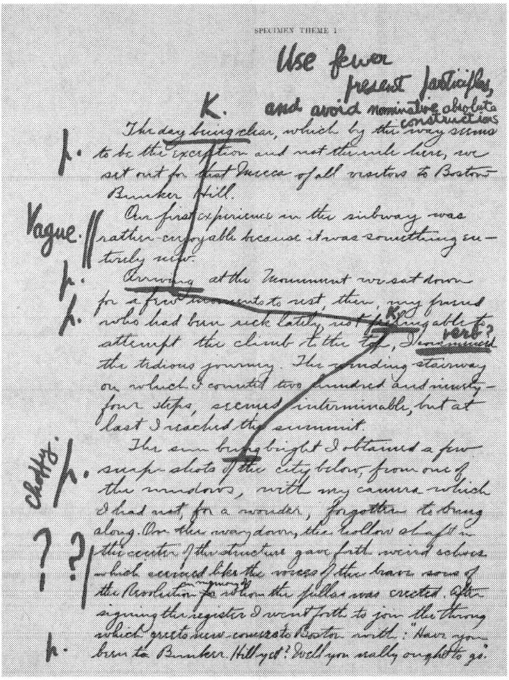

Figure 8-1

We have traditionally expected even our youngest writers to spell correctly, which makes no developmental sense. But we want to protect them from criticism—so we create word walls for them to copy from if they can't spell a word correctly. Looking back on my own career—as a writer for God's sake—I can locate times when I have been shamed for "bad grammar."

Several years ago, I was working with an editor on a brochure for a summer institute for teachers. Through some mishap, this editor introduced an error in the description of the course on boys' literacy that I was teaching—creating a really garbled sentence. Soon after the brochure came out, I found it pinned to the department bulletin board with the sentence circled and the comment, "Do you think a man or a woman wrote this sentence?"

I was shocked that anyone would publicly ridicule a program from our own department, and asked the Chair to send out a memo to the department expressing her concern and asking the person who wrote the comment to step forward. She commiserated with me but clearly did not think it was a big deal. I was overreacting. Neither did most of the faculty I talked to—it was as if I had it coming, or that pointing out errors was just normal operating procedure for an English

Department. In fact, Richard Lederer, one of our own PhDs, has made a living publishing humorous student errors. It's part of the culture.

One reason for this dislike of writing (particularly school writing) is the disparity between our ease of talking and the laborious work of writing. Mina Shaughnessy elegantly describes this contrast:

> The spoken language, looping back and forth between speakers, offering chances for groping and backing up and even hiding, leaving room for the language of hands and faces, of pitch and pauses, is generous and inviting. Next to this rich orchestration, writing is but a line that moves haltingly across the page, exposing as it goes all that the writer doesn't know, then passing into the hands of a stranger who reads it with a lawyer's eyes, searching for flaws. (1977, 7)

Plato in his dialogue *The Phaedrus* (1990) compares writing to sending out your child into the world, unprotected from misunderstanding and criticism. Unlike with talk, a text cannot speak back and correct misreadings, or restate to be clearer—it can "say only one and the same thing." Even experienced writers feel a loss of control when a manuscript goes into production.

The unprotected quality of writing, its separation and orphan quality, can pose dangers for the writer—from intercepted notes in class, to discovered diaries, to the exposure of politicians' emails, to the illegal possession of vernacular translations of the Bible in the sixteenth century. Even the most reasonable arguments on the Internet are vulnerable to hateful and anonymous comments, ones that the writers would never make in a face-to-face encounter.

Although we frequently view reading and writing as mirror processes, Deborah Brandt (2015) has argued that there are crucial differences, with writing often creating greater exposure. As one of the teacher consultants in our program regularly claimed, "Writing is like undressing in public." Another student, taking first-year writing through an open admission program, put it even more

my wrighting is the raw edge
of my soull. all the hate
and anger in me comes
out in it, that is why
I bear it, and I fear what
people will think of me
when I show them this side
of me.

Figure 8-2

forcefully in his jagged handwriting: "my wrighting is the raw edge of my soull. all the hate and anger in me comes out in it, that is why I fear it, and I fear what people will think of me when I show them this side of me" (Figure 8-2).

Still, with all its risks, we are becoming a writing culture. I'm not sure anyone would have predicted that the Internet, with all its visual affordances, would be such a site for writing. Where thirty years ago we had to worry about teaching student keyboarding, their fingers now dance on their iPhones—who would have thought thumbs could be so dexterous? Online chat rooms proliferate, the updating of Facebook profiles is constant, communities of young writers share fan fiction (there are approximately 750,000 posted pieces of fan fiction building off Harry Potter). No longer do writers have to pass through the editorial gatekeepers to make their writing public. The other day, I was in the checkout line at the grocery store, wearing my UNH English Department T-shirt. The young (nineteen at most) attendant asked what I taught and I replied writing. "Oh," she said, "I'm on my third novel."

But when we shift to the extended writing done in school, we are in a discomfort zone. A colleague of mine tells the story of being in Cincinnati for a composition conference, at the time of an NCAA regional basketball tournament. She found herself on the elevator with a six-foot, ten-inch young man. They introduced themselves, she a comp director, he a center for North Carolina. They chatted, and before they left the elevator the player commented, "You know, you're my worst nightmare."

A generation of great writing teachers has worked to rewrite the inner narratives that disable students and to open them to their own resources and to the endlessly generative possibilities of language.

In the rest of this chapter I will try to distill the work of my own career, trying to help us all tell a better, more generous story about the writing process.

Demystifying Writing—Or What I Learned from Don Murray

Feelings of anxiety and inadequacy arise when we have a deeply unrealistic understanding of the writing process. *And the very appearance of writing reinforces that lack of realism*. Take the text you are reading now. Sentences follow sentences, orderly, evenly spaced, seemingly inevitable. Nothing is crossed out, and there is no indicating mark like the Twitter icon to show where I took a break to check for notifications. There is no coffee image to mark where I stopped to brew a cup. And despite the length of this book, there is no indication of the short increments I wrote each day, an average of about 500 words. I could go on, but my point, an obvious one, is this: the continuity and uniformity of this written text totally obscures the fumbling and discontinuous act of writing it—when I read my own printed work it often seems like a smarter self wrote it.

Donald Murray, one-time paratrooper, winner of the Pulitzer Prize before he was thirty, and journalism teacher at the University of New Hampshire, helped demystify writing for generations of writers. He saw writing as a form of work, and felt a kinship to plumbers and carpenters and other laborers—it would not be unusual to see him in deep conversation with a tree service worker, a common sight in our neighborhood filled with tall and shallow-rooted white pines. He would be intrigued with how this tree cutter would decide on the sequence of the cutting. Or he might talk with long haul truckers about how they managed sleep on a long run.

He had no patience with the concept of "writer's block," which he felt was an affectation and excuse. A writer went to *work*, even if that work was at a desk in an office. After all, electricians don't experience "electrician's block," days on end when they can't seem to embrace wires and circuits. We are all laborers. He was also scathing about the idea of "talent," a fixed trait that supposedly you either had or didn't have. If such a thing existed, it could be outrun by those with productive attitudes and habits of writing. Maureen Barbieri, an award-winning writer and now an editor, recalls a comment by Don during her undergraduate days: "He was so reassuring. When I was an undergrad, he told me I had 'talent.' When I puffed out my chest, grinning, he said, 'It doesn't mean much. People like me get published because people like you sit on your hands.'"

Like any skill, we get better if we work at it regularly. There is a paradox here—as writers we want to do something different, unexpected, and original—but to do this most writers must create undeviating habits, often same time, same desk, same chair, same typeface, same margins, same lighting, same music, same writing tool, same length of writing session, same, same, same. Just as in meditation, the mind is opened to a receptive state—but only through a tightly prescribed procedure, a set of rituals that might involve breathing and body position. Unpredictability thus depends on predictability.

In my own experience, momentum is everything, one day's writing leading to the next. Murray would keep on hand laminated strips, about eight inches long, with the Latin maxim, "Nulla dies sine linea" (Never a day without a line) printed in thirty-six-point type. He would hand them out to anyone who expressed an interest in writing—teachers, students, janitors, receptionists, barmaids. One of these strips rests under the glass below my keyboard.

Nothing stalls the writing processes, kills fluency, of inexperienced writers more than perfectionism. (A Murray maxim: "The perfect is the enemy of the good.") For years I would ask my students early in a course to describe their writing processes. I remember the miserable time one young woman had with it. She would grip her pen tightly, write a few words, cross half of them out, stare out the window, squirm in her seat, crumple her paper, begin another, squirm in her seat, stare out the window, and so on.

After forty minutes, long after the other students had finished, she apologetically handed in her paper. It was 140 words long, written at an average of three and a half words per minute, about the typical rate of a first grader. Her pattern of cross-outs was probably the clearest example I have seen of the inhibiting power of perfectionism. Her first sentence was written as follows:

> ~~When I look back~~ courses focused
> My elementary and secondary English ~~classes~~ never ~~concer~~ on the
> elements of writing

The pattern of substitution is fascinating—most make marginal improvements. But at what an awesome price.

Another student described writing the first sentence of a paper on her grandfather:

> I decided to write about my grandfather. "Grandfather was a woodsman," I began. Was he? Actually he was also an apple picker and carpenter. I added those to the line. Now it was too long. I should concentrate on one subject, I said to myself. Was it *woodsman* or *woodsmen*? I looked it up in the dictionary. *Woodsman* was correct. I reread the first sentence; it sounded OK. Now for number 2.

The technical term for a process like this is *bleeding*. Bleeders seem to proceed painstakingly (and often painfully) word by word, sentence by sentence. And some of them are fine and productive writers, but my experience as writer and teacher convinces me that it is better to write more quickly, to outrun the censor—and leave editing and this woodman versus woodsmen stuff for editing.

That is the advice of poet William Stafford. One passage from his short essay "A Way of Writing" (1990) was so circulated and quoted in the UNH writing tribe that I will quote it at length. He identifies two attitudes that underlie his practice: one is receptivity, an uncritical openness to impressions, associations, an acceptance of what comes to him. The second attitude concerns "standards":

> I must be willing to fail. If I am to keep on writing, I cannot bother to insist on high standards. I must get into action and not let anything stop me, or even slow me much. By "standards" I do not mean "correctness"—spelling, punctuation, and so on. . . . I am thinking about what many people would consider "important" standards such as social significance, positive values, consistency, etc. I resolutely disregard these. Something better, greater is happening! I am following a process that leads so wildly and originally into new territory that no judgment can be made about values, significance, and so on. I am making something new, something that has not been judged before. (1990, 18)

Sometimes we shortened this elegant statement to a perverse form of advice: "To write well, you have to lower your standards." There is, after all, no gain to imposing standards that inhibit the act of writing—or that make us feel ashamed about what we are producing.

> To write well, you have to lower your standards.

And as long as we are dealing with paradoxes, here is another: the best way to reach an audience is to ignore it, at least early in the writing process. The best strategy is to concentrate on what you want to say, and if images of a critical audience obtrude into your consciousness, you will become excessively self-conscious, as my two first-year writers were. The great virtue of writing is that you can compose away from an audience; your first attempts are not seen or judged, and writers can use this separation to their advantage. Some of this early writing will need to be revised in later stages, when audience awareness should be a consideration. But we all have a better chance of appealing to an audience, of being successful, if we focus on what *we* want to say. My former colleague Gary

Lindberg, a noted literary scholar (and a belated member of the UNH writing tribe), describes his "heresy" this way:

> I do not consider what my prospective reader knows and still needs to know or what that reader's interests are. All my deliberation is reserved for the subject—*that* is what I manipulate and work out. I include as much as is necessary to make something clear *in itself* and coherent in its relations. And this frequently involves a mixture of what the reader knows and what is new. I flatter the reader by assuming he or she is enough like me to be interested in what *I* find interesting and demonstrate to be interesting. (1986, 190–191)

Lindberg's focal attention, his conscious effort, is spent on what he calls the "working out" ideas and relationships; that is, they require effort, though sometimes they come via inspiration ("through the backdoor"). But writers, he claims, can't solely survive on these gifts:

> Thoughts *do* arise unbidden . . . but they usually rise where we are looking for them. I tend to generate new ideas by questioning, by shifting contexts, by exploring relations, by puzzling, all quite deliberate activities. Some of my best insights do come while taking a bath, driving a car, sleeping, but I am not just sleeping, I'm sleeping *on* it, a deliberate gesture. (193)

But what is involved in this working out? That is clearly a mystery for inexperienced writers. The meager help that most are traditionally given is the outline, which tells nothing about the work *of* the writing, the elaborative and generative moves involved in composing, the discoveries and digressions and improvisations—in the end the pleasure of analytic writing.

I realize that *pleasure* and *analytic writing* are not often used in proximity. Particularly that version of writing we call "academic

> The best way to reach an audience is to ignore it, at least early in the writing process. The best strategy is to concentrate on what you want to say, and if images of a critical audience obtrude into your consciousness, you will become excessively self-conscious.

writing" is often synonymous with dullness, excessive length, boredom for readers, and drudgery for writers. In the vernacular of sports, *academic* is used to describe that part of the game when any effort is meaningless, as in "It's all academic now." And to be sure, some academic writing merits it, and some teaching practices promote it—to the point that students divide the world of writing into "creative" writing, which they find appealing, and school writing, which they do out of necessity. Like Dan Meyer in the previous chapter on math, I feel like I am selling something nobody wants to buy. But I am convinced that it doesn't have to be this way, and if we probe the "work" that Lindberg writes about, we can capture the *creativity of analysis.*

Moves

Let's start with this proposition: we teach students to play checkers, when they need to learn chess. In checkers all pieces have the same set moves, basically two—diagonal moves and jumps. That's it. In chess each piece has its own moves, creating an infinitely more complicated—and interesting—game. (OK you already know this.) But to analogize to writing, students are often shown only two moves—claim and evidence. These are significant, but by no means the total picture, and if all a student can do is claim and support, the writing often feels list-like and mechanical (and brief). When given an assignment longer than a couple pages, students invariably worry about meeting it—because they lack the tools of generation, the moves.

So what is a move in writing? We can start by putting aside the term *organization*. Organization implies something fixed, preformed, outlined, even static or formulaic. Moves, however, are options that we can take up in the process of writing—being alert to possibilities or, in Don Murray's terms, "expecting the unexpected." One of my colleagues, John Ernest, maybe the best teacher I have ever known, once said this about teaching: "You have to plan like hell—and then wing it." Without some plan or expectation, a writer (or teacher) can just drift and rely on luck—but "winging it" calls on our capacity to respond to what is happening, even when it means deviating from the plan. In other words, to improvise, you have to improvise *off something*. And the capacity to improvise, to be open to possibilities in the act of writing, is critical to analytic fluency.

One classic case of failing to improvise occurred during the Senate Watergate hearings in 1973. Many of the questioners were masterful, the great Sam Ervin of North Carolina and Howard Baker of Tennessee—brilliant and lucid lawyers. Yet one questioner on the panel, Joseph Montoya, was singularly ineffective. He had his set of questions, on note cards as I recall, and would move through them regardless of what the witness was saying. There was even a story, possibly an urban legend, that water use across the country spiked when he was doing the questioning, as we all took our bathroom breaks then.

So what is a "move"? I would define it as a shift in thought, as if the writer were responding to a question she or the reader might have. We make these moves in conversation all the time, and they are effortless because we have someone to prompt us ("What did you do next?" "You must be upset?" and so on). A writing conference, particularly one with an inexperienced writer, essentially models the prompts a more experienced writer does internally and automatically. The function of the conference is only secondarily to improve a particular piece of writing—if that is all it did the benefit would vanish instantly. Rather, the conference (or any response to writing) has lasting value if it models a set of questions or expectations, which the writer can, at some point internalize. None of us ever become fully self-sufficient at this; we always need another perspective to give us distance. But we can get better at it if we have internalized (and made automatic) a set of generative prompts.

There is not a new idea. In fact, one of the great and enduring contributions of classical rhetoric was the delineation of "topoi"—literally "places" a speaker could go to develop an argument. I list below what I believe are the prompts that I use as I write, and as I respond to student writing (and my own):

What is this about?

What happens next?

What does it look like, feel like, smell like?

How can I restate that?

What's my reaction to that?

What example or experience can I call up to illustrate that?

What parts of my prior reading can I bring to bear on that?

What comparison can I make that makes that clearer?

Why does that matter?

What do I mean by that?

Who else would agree with that? Disagree?

How can I qualify that statement? What are the exceptions?

How does that fit into larger debates or controversies?

Clearly it is essential to maintain a focus in writing—staying on track, maintaining what one of my colleagues calls a "line" that threads through and connects the parts of the text that creates a sense of continuity, of flow. But it is possible to be too linear, to create a monologue that is too unvaried.

These are my chess moves. As I write I sometimes feel that there is a beacon in my head, something like you would find on a lighthouse, or a search light, that scans what I know, have done, have read, have seen—to make connections. This light is moving even when I am not writing, and at times, when I am really obsessed, I can't find the switch to turn it off.

Clearly it is essential to maintain a focus in writing—staying on track, maintaining what one of my colleagues calls a "line" that threads through and connects the parts of the text that creates a sense of continuity, of flow. But it is possible to be too linear, to create a monologue that is too unvaried. The side trips, the shifts, repetitions, humorous digressions, anecdotes, asides, multiple voices—all have their place too. We don't necessarily maintain the reader's attention (or our own interest in writing) by relentlessly marching forward with claim and evidence. The argument needs to be leavened by story, seriousness by humor, the abstract by the concrete. And all of these shifts create a sense of motion and rhythm that sustain attention.

The most eloquent advocate for digression is, of course, Holden Caulfield in *The Catcher in the Rye*, who describes an "Oral Expression" class where students gave speeches and the audience was encouraged to yell "digression" when they got off their topics. Holden describes what happened to one very shy student, Richard Kinsella, who got a D+ on a speech about his family farm in Vermont—because he had not described "what kind of animals and vegetables and stuff grew on the farm and all":

> What he did was, Richard Kinsella, he'd *start* telling you about all that stuff—then all of a sudden he'd start telling you about this letter his mother got from his uncle, and how his uncle got polio and all when he

was forty-two years old, and how he wouldn't let anybody come to see him in the hospital because he didn't want anybody to see him with a brace on. It didn't have much to do with the farm—I admit it—but it was *nice.* It's nice when somebody tells you about their uncle. Especially when they start out telling you about their father's farm and then all of a sudden get more interested in their uncle. I mean it's dirty to keep yelling "Digression" at him when he's all nice and excited. (Salinger 1951, 239)

When Holden's teacher, Mr. Antolini, asks him if he doesn't think it matters if students stick to the point, Holden replies: "Oh, sure. I like somebody to stick to the point. But I don't like them to stick *too* much to the point" (238).

One of my colleagues, Tomasen Carey, artfully connects writing with dramatic improvisation. She is a big fan of props—extravagant hats, boas, jewelry—which she carries in a box to many of her classes. For a long time I just thought it was her drama thing, and didn't appreciate how central it was to her teaching. There was a joke that I evaded classes where she brought her box out. But one time, at a staff meeting, I was trapped. The box came out and there was no escape.

As I recall I was given a flowery hat, scarf, and ukulele. We put on the clothes and wrote a monologue that the character would say. Somehow the experience of having the clothes *on* made a huge difference. I became this woman I imagined, a widow, and the ukulele belonged to her deceased husband. It brought back memories to her, of the time they met in college, the jug band he played with—one of their favorite songs was "The Eggplant That Ate Chicago":

It landed in Chicago

Thought Chicago was a treat

It was sweet

It was just like candy

She remembered how he would sing the corniest songs to the accompaniment of this ukulele, and she would put on the "not again" look. But she loved it—and missed it. It all came back to her.

After we wrote, we read our writing, with the costume still on, using the voice of our character. We were freed from ourselves in the way fiction writers often talk about. We could unselfconsciously inhabit another character. I could be this woman. It all made sense now.

Inner Speech and Writing

When I began my career at the University of New Hampshire, Don Murray was publishing a series of important essays on the writing process—and in them he would often portray the emerging text as virtually a cocreator. It all seemed very mystical to me. Don urged us to "listen" to the text, to pay attention to the "informing line." At the time, I could accept that there was a cognitive process—in my head—that was creating the writing. But it seemed a metaphoric fantasy to claim a role for the text in shaping and creating the writing. That was what *I* was doing. The writing wasn't doing the writing.

I now think he was right, and this insight into composing was one of his greatest gifts to us. But it took me a circuitous route to get to this point, one that passed through the great Russian psychologist Lev Vygotsky (as so many great ideas do), via Linda Flower's classic essay on "writer-based prose." In *Thought and Language* (1986), Vygotsky describes "inner speech," the abbreviated language we use in our heads to think, language that works to do that thinking but is not fully communicative to readers or listeners. For example, one feature of inner speech is that it focuses on the predicate and not the subject—a source of persistent confusion in my own marriage. Out of the blue, I say something like, "This is going to be hard to explain to the community." (Talking about some school board matter.) And she says, understandably, "*What* is going to be hard to explain?" That subject is so familiar to me that it doesn't need expression (to me)—it is the "hard to explain" part that is the *new* part of my thinking. These unidentified pronouns have been a minor strain on our marriage.

Another feature of inner speech is *saturation*, language that serves as a placeholder for associations, feelings, stories. Suppose I wrote the "simple" sentence:

> I grew up in Ashland, Ohio.

For a reader, this may simply identify a small town in Ohio, or more explicitly an exit off US 71 if they have done any driving in the state—that's it. But for me the very name evokes my whole childhood; learning to swim at the Y, our house on Broad Street with the big yard that was a magnet for all the kids in the neighborhood, milkshakes at the Boyer Dairy Bar, the great flood of 1969 after which Ashland was declared a "disaster area," and my friend Tom McNaull's comment, "It's about time."

If I am responsive to the name of my hometown, it opens up my memory—just as the idea of "farm" was connected by Richard Kinsella to a memory of his uncle. So when we "listen to the text," what I suspect we are doing is connecting with episodic memories, stories, evoked by these saturated, deeply resonant words.

For example, earlier in this chapter I used the expression "the elaborative and generative moves involved in composing, the discoveries and digressions and improvisations." The word *improvisations* evoked jazz musicians and improv comedians—and it occurred to me I could interview them to see how they "listen" and build off a riff or a prompt. The greatest jazz album of all time, Miles Davis' *Kind of Blue*, was recorded with almost no planning. A couple of hours before the recording Davis created some opening chords, which he presented to the musicians at the beginning of the recording—all of which sounds terrifying to me. Could I interview some jazz musicians to have them describe this process, analogous to the one I am writing about?—something I've always been curious about. Again, even if I don't do that for this book, it is in the memory bank.

Making this kind of lateral, unexpected, move, evoked by a single word, requires an essential form of openness that a writer needs to cultivate—Murray's "listening to the text." As the great (and somewhat crazy) British novelist Laurence Sterne wrote about his process: "my work is digressive, and it is progressive too,—and at the same time" (1965, 54). And the trigger, the prompt, for these digressions is often a key saturated word. If all we teach students is the progressive part, that march through the outline, they may not develop the generative capability to really explore a topic.

My premise is that the main problem for inexperienced writers is not correctness or organization—it is fluency. And this lack of fluency—when compared to our oral facility—causes them to produce writing that falls embarrassingly short of what we would like to convey. Writing is bleeding, drop by drop—and bears no resemblance to the student's otherwise talkative and articulate self. Take this one paragraph from a five-paragraph essay on an admired person, written by an eleventh grader:

> My mother has had a very **hard life** and sometimes I do not understand how she can take the **pressure** any longer. When she gets really **upset** we talk and I try to understand.

I have bolded three terms that feel to me like they are saturated, that they serve the writer as placeholders for powerful experiences—and they can serve as a thread that could lead the writer to rich episodic memories, family stories, that could be added. As teachers we might prompt a student like this to follow that thread—perhaps to pick out words that she thinks she can say more about. Or, in the case of this paragraph, to gently prompt: "I'd like to get a clearer picture of that pressure she is under, can you tell me more about that."

Too often with writing like this, we might write *expand* in the margins, but I am convinced that the writer needs to *hear* the expansion, to expand orally; otherwise she has no sense of what she might say to expand. As Vygotsky (once again) argues, this mental operation of expansion occurs socially, in conversation with a teacher or other reader, before it goes underground and becomes "intrapersonal."

This process of writing feels to me more musical than logical. By that I mean music is often built around some motif or theme that the composer plays with. The motif is altered, the key changes, the motif is carried by different instruments, it is inverted, at different tempos—it may be contested by another motif that feels emotionally different. These may not even be the exact musical terms, but that is the feeling I get—there is repetition with variation. In writing this book, I felt that I have not so much a thesis as a motif—the performative risks we take as learners—and the task for me was not to argue for it, but to *play it out*, to open it up. The root meaning of essay is "trial" or "test" and I have tried to do just that with my germ of a beginning.

I realize that it may seem like I am supporting overwriting, and I am. Almost all the good writers I have encountered went through a stage where they wrote at length: long stories in middle school, space stories with endless chapters. They pushed description and dialogue and plot to the limit, often boring to any outside reader. It's the same with athletes—watch promising middle school athletes. They will often charge into a hopeless layup, dive for a ball clearly out of reach, attempt the impossible pass. Often their bodies are not under full control. Yet that daring, that excess, that lack of caution, is a virtue. Good coaches know that. Control will come later. In the same way, the overwriter can be taught to control the gift of excess, but the under-writer has no awareness that this excess is even a possibility.

"Always the First Person That Is Speaking"

Teaching students to avoid the first person is one of the great crimes of writing instruction. It is alienating and forces students into intensely awkward expressions, passives, and having to refer to themselves in the third person. Students are fed the lie that they should avoid *I think* because the reader knows it is their thinking. But any sixth grader knows these two sentences are not equivalent:

> I think you need a haircut.
>
> You need a haircut.

The second is more declarative, the first more hedged—this is my opinion. To this point I have used *I* 129 times (counting those I quoted) in this chapter so far (and counting), and I (131) see little point in expecting my students to write more formally than I am doing now, or than editorial writers for the *New York Times* do.

In writing, as in teaching, our personality is our greatest asset. Not that we can simply be ourselves—personality is a tool that can be used deliberately. Our sense of humor, our enthusiasm, our energy, even our quirks, these are potentially some of our greatest strengths. The same holds for writing—it is terrible advice to withhold or suppress these human attractions.

The prohibition of *I* is based on another patent myth: that the writer must present himself or herself as objective, and the use of *I* calls attention to possible bias of the writer—when in fact, bias is inevitable, even desirable. As writers we can perhaps be reasonable, but objectivity, some view from nowhere, is not really possible, at least for mortal human beings. Henry David Thoreau's take on this issue at the beginning of *Walden*:

> In most books, the *I*, or first person is omitted; in this it will be retained; that in respect to egotism, is the main difference. We commonly do not remember that it is, after all, always the first person that is speaking. (2000, 39)

All writing is personal. That is, to be effective the writer has to locate some personal stake in it; otherwise the process is self-alienating.

Thoreau goes on to make a powerful analogy that should be posted in every writing class in the country:

> Moreover, I, on my side, require of every writer, first or last, a simple and sincere account of his own life, and not merely what he has heard of other men's lives; such an account as he would send to his kindred from a distant land; for if he has lived sincerely, it must have been in a distant land from me. (39)

All writing, then, is travel writing. A student has been to some other land, maybe literally—an actual place; or more generally a family, a relationship, a loss, or an experience reading a book or poem. And as readers, our central questions are simply: "What's it like?" "Where have you been?" That curiosity sustained me through my career as a writing teacher. Some topics, death of grandparents, even parents, were visited often, but it was still a different country each time, and my question was, "What's it like, *for you*?"

In his book, *The Sense of Style* (2014), Steven Pinker describes the "classic style," which seems consistent with Thoreau's invitation to travel writing. The writer in the classic style is not writing up or down to an audience—but to a peer, interested, someone who has not seen what you have seen. This part about *seeing* is crucial, as Pinker reminds us that a huge part of our brains, about a quarter, is involved in sight. We are good at it, and depend on it. Some versions of academic writing ignore this, and without any visual referents, it's tough going. Try on a couple sentences from one of the journals in my field:

> This extension of the political to include the ideological, however, is itself an ideology in conflict with a prevailing ideology. In this prevailing ideology, the ideological is seen precisely as false consciousness; the political is restricted to either statecraft or the machinations for pursuing private interests; and ideology, politics, and power are, if sometimes necessary, nonetheless always dirty. (Horner 2000, 122)

Tired? And that's only two sentences. So many abstractions, and the dizzying repetition of *ideology*, with only one visual referent (*dirty*).

By contrast the writer in the classic style is "directing the reader to something in the world she can see for herself. All eyes are on an agent: a protagonist, a mover, a shaker, a driving force" (Pinker 2014, 48). The classic style is story driven, with "real characters doing things, rather than by naming an abstract concept that encapsulates those events in a single word" (49) (like *ideology*).

Pinker is clear that this style does not avoid ideas, but it finds a dramatic and visual language for conveying them. And although it sounds pompous to say that I try to write in the classic style (in my chalet overlooking Lake Como), I have never felt comfortable with some of the conventions of academic writing, and I am drawn to this visual style. In the following paragraph, which opens a chapter on teacher research, I try to set up the tension between traditional educational research that presumes to establish universal principles, and the chaos and particularity of individual classroom settings.

> In Lorrie Moore's short story, "Real Estate," the main character reflects on marriage: "Marriage, she felt, was a fine arrangement generally, except one never got it generally. One got it very, very specifically."
>
> The same holds for teaching; whatever theories and research base we have as we enter a classroom, we are very quickly overrun with the particularities of the work—with the personalities of students, the established curriculum, the dynamics of friendship groups, the school schedule, the specials, interruptions, one's relationship to the principal and other authorities, the space and environment of the classroom ("can anyone adjust the damn heat?"). Not to mention the personal baggage we bring in—our passions, personality, hesitancies, the sense of our own teaching style and limitations. In this welter of interacting "variables," if we can even use that term, it is easy to feel that research and theory are purified, rarified, remote and unresponsive to the realities of teaching—which we all experience "very, very specifically." (Newkirk 2015, 211)

I try to use these cascading lists to create a visceral sense of chaos and particularity, building the list off a Lorrie Moore quote that I love, and then recapture at the end. It is also an example of one of my guiding tendencies—*juxtaposition*, connecting different genres of information (short story and educational writing).

If all writing is travel writing, this visual style is most amenable to taking readers on the trip, and I feel it is an attractive style for students. After all, we indirectly acknowledge the primacy of vision when we say, "I see what you mean."

Two Last Bits of Advice

While I still have the floor, I want to offer two bits of advice that might help when we undertake major writing projects, on which it is so easy to lose faith and momentum. On a big project it is essential to "think small." It is easy to be intimidated by its complexity and the demand it places on us. The antidote is to break that bigger project into a series of manageable pieces. When I do sit down to write, I am not writing the "book," only the next few paragraphs, the next increment, the next small installment. I learned this lesson, for good, one summer when I was a lifeguard at the Brookside Pool in Ashland, Ohio.

Bob Doerr, another lifeguard and distance swimmer on our high school team, would sometimes swim the entire length of the fifty-meter pool underwater. He'd con kids into betting small change that he couldn't do it. One day I decided to try it during lunch break, and I asked him for any advice. "Don't look up," he said, "the end is so far away. It will psych you out. Watch the bottom of the pool. That's the secret."

So I tried it, following his advice. I locked my neck in position and watched the bottom and could see the progress I was making. Even as I went into oxygen debt, I kept looking at the bottom, until I came to the cross that marked the end of the lane, looked up, and was at the wall. This swim, these fifty seconds, became a parable for me, a story that my poor graduate students have heard numerous times. "Don't look up. Forget the whole project. Focus on the next step, the next manageable step. What's next?"

I have also come to an understanding of preparation—so valuable, but you can only prepare so much. At some point you have to dive in and trust you can find the way. At some point, usually before I plan on writing, I ask, "What do I have in the tank? How far can I drive?" With fingers literally shaking I create a file, "Chapter 1," and start. There will always be more you could have done, more research, more interviews, longer lists, a more complex web. We are never truly ready, not for anything big and complex. We are never ready to be husbands and wives, parents, teachers. We have to be ready to learn on the way.

How well I recall the moment when we left the hospital and we took our first child, my daughter Sarah, home. I'm thinking, "Holy shit, you're letting us do this? I had to take a test to drive a car, but you are letting us take this baby, this human being, home." I had attended all the birth classes, but there was no way I was ready for this. I was petrified putting on those first diapers, afraid I would stick my daughter with a pin. I didn't know exactly how to hold her, what her cries meant.

We are never truly ready, not for anything big and complex. We have to be ready to learn on the way.

But I learned. I paid attention, tried things, and Sarah let us know what worked. After a while I could distinguish the hunger cry from the diaper cry from the tired cry. I learned to rock her on my shoulder as I walked, so she would go to sleep. I learned to read *her.*

Similarly, in any long writing project I have learned to trust the process, the unfolding. I am prepared to a point. I may have a crude chapter outline, claims I want to make, stories I want to tell, student papers I want to quote. But, primarily, the project teaches me how to do the project. I try to pay attention to what I am doing, to be present, to be alert to the possibilities that open before me, to take detours now and then. Invariably, the research I need becomes apparent in the actual writing.

I cannot totally silence the voices that discourage me. ("This is obvious." "It's been said before." "Who will really read this?") I cannot avoid periods of what Peter Elbow calls "nausea"—becoming sick of my own project, a trap for all writers, I think. But I can counter these shaming voices with other voices in my head.

I can replay John Keats in his letter to his brother Tom, in which he describes a "negative capability": "when a man is capable of being in uncertainties, mysteries, doubts, without any irritable reaching after fact and reason" (1899, 277). It's OK to stay with uncertainty, doubts, and to work your way through them and not panic or get "irritable." I can replay Laurence Sterne who has this to say about digression:

> For, if he is a man of the least spirit, he will have fifty deviations from a straight line to make with this or that party as he goes along, which he can no ways avoid. He will have views and prospects to himself perpetually soliciting his eye, which he can no more help standing still to look at than he can fly. (1965, 28)

Sterne gives me permission to be open to unexpected possibilities, and to go off track at times, to write with "spirit." I, of course, hear my mentor and former neighbor, Don Murray, who brings me back to earth with this declaration: "Writing is not primarily a matter of talent, of dedication, of vision, of vocabulary, of style, but simply the matter of sitting." It's the work.

But more than anything, I hear the haunting last line of Theodore Roethke's poem, "The Waking":

> I learn by going where I have to go.

I think of it whenever I have something difficult to do. If I keep moving forward, even in the dark, I can find my way.

IV
VOICES

CHAPTER 9

Learning to Fail Publicly

What We All Can Learn from Athletes and Coaches

The better stories we have, the faster swimmers we are going to have.

—**LEA MAURER,** OLYMPIC CHAMPION SWIMMER AND FORMER WORLD-RECORD HOLDER

A story about sports and language.

In my sophomore year in high school I was a member of the cross-country team. I joined mainly to get ready for track season, but I came to love the early fall practices on the town's golf course—and looked forward to the first meet on the grounds of Worthington High School, north of Columbus. As I recall, the course began in a big open lawn in front of the school and went toward the expansive athletic fields. After about a quarter mile it plunged down a steep hill onto a long flat stretch.

As the gun went off I felt myself propelled by the mass of runners, almost sprinting across that open area—by the time I reached the hill I was beginning to breath heavily, and the charge down the hill felt completely uncontrolled, my arms wind milling. Within minutes I was gasping for breath, panicked; I slowed down, as runners passed me in waves. I tried to regain my breath but couldn't keep from gasping for air—with a good mile and a half to go. I slowed to a walk.

I dropped to one knee—a race official then came over to me to ask me how I was doing and to walk me off the course.

I still vividly recall the feeling of defeat, embarrassment, and shame that overwhelmed me at that moment. I had *quit*. I was therefore a *quitter*. It was the only story I could tell myself about that race, the only explanation I could come up with ("A winner never quits and a quitter never wins."). I truly believed that my problem was a deep flaw in character or willpower—I wasn't cut out for this sport (though I ran well in practice). I could feel my coach's disapproval and disappointment when I told him. We didn't talk about it, and I'm not sure I would have known how to explain it, or he would have known how to help.

In retrospect I could imagine a different outcome. If my coach and I had thought about it together, or I had written about it then (and not just now, fifty-two years later), I might have come to a different and less self-condemning conclusion. We might have gotten past the shame of the moment to realize that I had simply made a serious mistake in pacing (and probably a failure to warm up properly). It was, after all, my first race and my first time away from the familiarity of my home course. My difficulty was not the result of a lack of willpower or flawed character, but the physiological effect of these mistakes—ones that could be corrected in future races.

We might have developed a strategy to determine the best early pace for me, one that would allow me to even accelerate in the latter parts of the race. As I began to feel comfortable in that early pace, I could gradually have made it faster and moved toward a more even pace in subsequent races. In other words, I could learn to take control and avoid that desperate feeling of complete breathlessness.

But we need a language to do this reflection; we need something more than the rough, macho code of winners and losers. As it turned out, those eight or nine minutes on the Worthington course haunted my experience in cross-country.

All my life I have been fascinated by athletes who fail publicly and refuse to give up on—or even doubt—themselves. Mired in a hitting slump, they still hold their head high after a strikeout; they don't throw their bat, or curse. They take their seat on the bench, but what goes through their minds? How do they process this difficulty, this setback—without dwelling on it in unproductive ways, as I did with my cross-country embarrassment?

This chapter gave me the chance to talk to people who could answer these questions—professional athletes, coaches, athletic counselors—the ones who sit down with the pass receiver who dropped the "easy" pass that would have won the game, the runner who dropped the relay baton. I started with Rich Kent, a gifted teacher and coach and the author of a wonderful book, *Room 109*, which described his work at Mountain Valley High School in Rumford, Maine. He coached a championship high school soccer team, mentored Olympic class skiers, and has recently published a series of books on using writing in journals and notebooks to help athletes, in his words, become "students of the game." I visited him in his family home in Rumford, a mill town with plumes of smoke from the paper mills visible from miles away. We spoke in his dining room, which is dominated by a huge Brad Washburn photo of Burt's Ravine on the western side of Mount Washington—named after Rich's great grandfather.

I began by asking him about an embarrassing experience as a coach, and he instantly recalled a painful loss early in his career:

> As a coach I took an undefeated soccer team from Rumford—we were only in our second year as a team—to the state championship playoff game. We went to the big city to play against Cheverus High School. I had no background to prepare my athletes for what this team would be like. We thought that being undefeated, we were all set for what was going to happen.
>
> By the time the score was 5–0, the kids were embarrassed and just sort of barely functioning on the field—and I was about in shock. On the bus back to Rumford we had kids weeping. And I was still kind of, "What in the world just happened?" I didn't have a full picture of the other team. I didn't have a clear picture of where we stood in the soccer world in Maine.
>
> So I let the team down. And that for me turned into a quintessential lesson in how to talk to athletes about the larger picture of performance. I could have told them the truth, that Cheverus was an older and talented team, more talented than we were. The way to prepare against a team like that might have been to take a defensive stance, drag back five or six players, go for a counterattack goal. I could tell a story of how the game might unfold—and, in the end, if it doesn't work it doesn't work. Having a larger picture of the game, being a student of the game and themselves, calms those embarrassing moments, and grounds them in what happened.

The way to become a "student of the game" or to get the "larger picture of the game" is to use language, to create what Kent calls a "narrative." By narrative he does not mean an anecdote or amusing story, but an explanation, drained of the emotionalism that comes in the moment. It can be retrospective (How did I get to this point?), immediate (What is happening in this game?), or prospective (What can we expect? How can we visualize the game ahead?).

His insights are, as the earlier story indicates, hard-earned and derived from his own experiences, successes, and failures. But they have strong psychological backing. Martin Seligman (1998), former president of the American Psychological Association, has done pioneering work on what he calls "explanatory styles." The ways in which we explain difficulty has huge implications for psychological—and even physical—health. His work in this area anticipates Carol Dweck's delineation of the growth mindset (she herself did important work here in the 1990s).

An unhealthy explanatory style has three characteristics. When confronted with a setback or failure, it is possible to see the cause as only *internal* ("I am fully responsible for what happened. It is entirely the result of a personal deficiency."); as *global* ("I'm just not good at math/sports/etc."); and as *permanent* ("That's just the way I am. I can't really change this."). In extreme cases, this style of explanation is termed "learned helplessness" and is associated with depression and other physical ailments.

Of course, stated like this, the pathology of this style of thinking is obvious. The problem is that in the moment of defeat and failure—when people start toward the exits halfway through your talk, when every soccer pass misses its mark, when you get a D on the test you studied hard for—in these cases, there is a hollow feeling in the gut, frustration, pain, anger, embarrassment, a feeling of being small and inadequate. I don't think we can bypass this emotionalism, except, perhaps, by not caring in the first place. Our body reacts before our mind has a chance, and if our mind cannot process and convert these feelings, it's hard to get beyond them. The great cognitive psychological Marvin Minsky put it this way:

> Thinking is a process, and if your thinking does something you don't want it to you should be able to say something microscopic and analytical about it, not something enveloping and evaluating about yourself as a learner. The important thing in refining your thought is to try to depersonalize your interior: it may be all right to deal with other people in a vague global way, but it is devastating if this is the way you deal with yourself. (Quoted in Bernstein 1981, 122)

One way to "depersonalize the interior" and to be "microscopic and analytical" is to invert the explanatory principles associated with learned helplessness:

- Our failures are usually not entirely due to personal deficiencies (like not trying). Often we find ourselves in situations we are not prepared for, or situations where the chance of success is small (e.g., Kent's game with Cheverus). It's not all on us. We have to be fair to ourselves.
- When we have a setback, we need to be able to pinpoint the exact reason for it, to avoid the "vague global" explanations about our general lack of ability in a certain area. If a lesson went flat and students lost attention, where did I lose them? Did I get too technical and confusing at some point?
- If we can localize a problem, we can do something about it. I can't help myself if I decide I am not a good lecturer. But I can improve if I can locate an ineffective section of my PowerPoint.

Rich Kent (2012) promotes this explanatory style, being a student of the game, through a dazzling array of prompts that have been used by elite coaches and athletes (his book on swimming notebooks comes with an endorsement from one of my heroes, the mighty Matt Grevers, six-time Olympic medalist!). The prompts ask athletes to think about their preparation for a season and their goals, personal and team. Athletes break down any athletic performance—in a swim race, the warm-up, start, turns, pacing, finish.

I am always struck by how instinctive this type of thinking is among top performers. I was recently watching the final laps of the 2016 Daytona 500. Dale Earnhardt Jr., a favorite to win the race, was in the cluster of cars (going more than 190 miles an hour), when his car suddenly veered left, narrowly missing being broadsided, crashed into a retaining wall (eerily similar to the crash that killed his dad), ripping up the infield as it came to a stop. Earnhardt was unhurt, crawled out of the car, and almost immediately was interviewed. He calmly explained that handling had been hard all day, one cause being the warmer weather—no histrionics, no throwing of the helmet. "We have some adjustments to make."

To put it another way, failure makes us vulnerable to a stress reaction: we feel vulnerable and threatened, exposed. We can feel it in our bodies (think of your computer crashing). We can lash out, find someone to blame, feel helpless. The ability to calm ourselves in the face of difficulty is a key feature of resilience, which is built on a history of calm, consistent responses from caregivers, beginning in infancy (especially in infancy). This enabling history effectively prepares the body to react to this potentially threatening situation with a signal that says: "You are safe. Life is going to be fine. Let down your guard; people around you will protect and provide for you" (Tough 2016, 60). This self-calming allows the learner to slow down, consider problems more carefully, focus attention longer, and receive (and even seek) help. Virtually all of Rich Kent's writing prompts work to put his athletes in this space.

His most compelling examples come from his own work with soccer players. One of the prompts invites athletes to identify the strengths of the opposing team after a game and write a letter to the coach. Here is what one of his players wrote after a loss:

> Dear Coach:
>
> You have a great team. They are disciplined and organized and the kids were good guys even though they kicked our butts! Your players had wicked good talk. They supported each other with talk. . . . At tonight's match I could see that. I was impressed how your midfielders used their defenders so well. They got out of a lot of trouble with quick back passes. I also thought your one and two touch passes were *useful* as our coach says. We learned a lot today and I am proud of the way we played even though we lost 3-1. Someday I hope our team will play like yours. Good luck with the rest of the season.
>
> Yours,
> Kevin (Tough 2012, 66)

What a contrast from emotional meltdowns (or blaming the refs).

Kent acknowledges that his approach is resisted by "Old World coaches" who want only one narrative, theirs, to account for a win or loss.

> We need to ask student athletes, "What is the story of this match and how did it end up the way it did in your eyes?" You have a story to tell and the other 10 people have a story to tell and the coach has his or her story to tell, and the next day you get together and you tell these stories out loud—and then you ask how can we build on this understanding.

To be sure, he acknowledges (and loves) the full range of emotions of a contest—it is one of the attractions of all sports. But writing and reflecting creates "balance." It becomes, in John Dewey's terms, an "experience," with the one key trait of an experience being that it *leads*, it is instructive, it allows us to experiment with the future and not just let it happen to us.

Kent's athletic prompts are simply versions of the prompts he used in his portfolio-focused classroom. Students were constantly monitoring their progress, self-assessing, and writing letters of commentary on the work of their peers. For any difficult task it is productive to consider questions like:

- How well am I prepared to do this project? What key things do I need to do to get ready?
- What challenges or difficulties do I expect to face in doing it? How can I get help in dealing with these?
- What do I find interesting or engaging in this project?
- What is the key thing I want to learn in this project?

Writing and reflecting creates "balance." It becomes, in John Dewey's terms, an "experience," with the one key trait of an experience being that it *leads*, it is instructive, it allows us to experiment with the future and not just let it happen to us.

When we ask these questions we become students of the game—whatever that game is.

Lavorare di più

The office of Tim Churchard, sports psychology coach for the UNH hockey and football teams, is like a museum. Tim has been involved in UNH sports since the mid-1960s when he played fullback—and one of the pictures on his wall is an old clipping of him charging into the line in a game against the University of Connecticut. "I show them that picture to remind them what a small precious moment their sports career is. That was my moment."

He made a special point of showing me a reproduction of a painting of an older African American teaching his grandson (one supposes) the banjo. "This has everything you need to know about education. There is love there, physical connection—the kid is sitting in his lap. There is food, and education is always best with food. But the most important thing is this—the *kid's* hands are on the banjo. I need to track down the original. It's in Pennsylvania somewhere."

I raised with Tim the problem of coping with a mistake—how do athletes learn not to dwell on it, particularly if it was a crucial one in a game? He noted that this is a particular issue for goalies, kickers, and quarterbacks ("Without them I'd be out of business"):

> You have to be like the old Etch A Sketch. You have to be able to clear your mind. I teach them meditation—you've got to have an empty mind that reflects only what goes on in the present. I have them come up with a trigger word that communicates to the mind that it's just play. Take Ty Conklin [an All American UNH goalie]. If a goal went in, he had to concentrate on the next shot or that would go in too. Goalies get it. And he used to bang his stick on each post—bang bang . . . bang bang. And he would repeat, "Next shot. Next shot." He had to say it, not think it. And later on I was watching him with the Detroit Red Wings and a goal goes in and he does the bang bang—so he took it to the pros.

Tim, a longtime friend, always struck me as a fascinating hybrid—tough guy and mystic, part Mike Ditka, part Dalai Lama.

Churchard had a lot to say about the mistakes coaches make correcting mistakes:

> Over and over again I hear from players: "They never miss when I am screwing up, but they always miss when I do something good." But if you follow a whole game or practice you'll see them do extraordinary things. You'll also see them screw up. But what do coaches zero in on? We zero in on what went wrong and assume they know that they do things right or they wouldn't be playing. But they don't know. They don't have that confidence, especially at that age. They may look like men, but in many ways they are still boys. The best time to correct a kid is when they are doing something right. And you say, "That's the way you should do it every time. Put that in your head." You don't focus on what the kid does wrong because that's what they will focus on.

"The best time to correct a kid is when they are doing something right. And you say, 'That's the way you should do it every time. Put that in your head.' You don't focus on what the kid does wrong because that's what they will focus on."

This sounded identical to the advice my own writing mentor Donald Murray pounded into my head: *build from strengths*.

Visualizing is a key to more consistent effective play. According to Churchard, "They need to visualize themselves doing it right. The whole secret of visioning is you see yourself doing it right over and over again in slow motion."

I asked Churchard to give me an example of visualizing for goalies:

> Say tonight I'm going to work on the five-hole [the opening between the pads]. So they're going to see themselves with a guy bearing down on them and they are watching his eyes. They're going to see themselves pulling their pads together—see themselves squaring their pads to the shooter. They see the puck coming in slow motion and caroming off the pads. They see themselves doing this over and over. That programs the muscles to react.

I recently watched the sixty-meter dash finals for the SEC conference, and the winner, Christian Coleman, was asked if he was surprised he won. "No," he answered, "I'd seen it happen in my mind."

By the end of our talk, I felt like I was tapping in to Tim's best motivational stories. He often has to deal with athletes who were stars at their high schools or prep schools and find themselves struggling to make the fourth line in college. They were regulars on the power play, but not at this new level. They're frustrated, and Tim asks them to draw a circle.

> I tell them to put inside the circle all the things that they can control. And on the outside the things they can't control. They can't control their playing minutes or whether they are on the power play. That's the coach's decision. That's on the outside. But they can control their work ethic. They can convince a goalie to stay after practice so they can work on their shot. They can control their attitude. That's on the inside. And you can always work harder.
>
> A guy I know, Rock Perdoni, was captain of the Georgia Tech football team. He was born in Italy and he became an outstanding defensive lineman, a Lombardi finalist. But for a long time the team wasn't performing, and he spoke to his dad about it, in Italian: "I'm frustrated. I don't know what to do. I'm the captain and I'm responsible."
>
> Now his dad didn't know much about football, actually he hated football, loved soccer. But he said to him, "Work harder. *Lavorare di più*. You can always work harder. It's always an option for you whether you're laying bricks or playing football." So he started staying after practice, hitting sleds, and after a while the other captains joined him. And then he said to the seniors, "I want you out there." And pretty soon the whole team was out there, for fifteen minutes, every player, no coaches—and they started winning games. You have to find things that can work for you and that you can control.

Like Rick Kent, Churchard sees writing as key—athletes need an "action plan," specific actions that they can work on to improve. "You know the term I hate, 'snake bitten.' It's such a cop out. You need to make a plan, be specific, draw the damn circle."

I thought I would try this question of coping with failure on arguably the best athlete to come from our community, Sam Fuld. As a young baseball player he was so good that he wasn't allowed to play with kids his own age. He went on to Stanford where he set records in the College World Series, then on to a professional career with the Chicago Cubs, Tampa Bay Rays, and the Oakland Athletics. There are YouTube highlights compilations of his great catches, including one where he seems to momentarily disappear into the vines of Wrigley Field after a catch, then quickly pivot to double up the runner at first. When he was with Tampa Bay he was able to live out a dream and play in Fenway Park against the team he followed as a kid—the Boston Red Sox—in a nationally televised game. He went four for five with a home run, triple, and two doubles—in other words he would have accomplished the notoriously difficult "cycle" if he had stopped at first on one of his doubles. Like I say, a legend.

Yet he was a streaky hitter in the majors, and sometimes his inconsistency edged him out of a regular starting position. Here is his response:

> The discouragement and frustration that come with failure is inevitable. There's not a single professional athlete who isn't negatively affected, at least to some degree, by poor performance. How we deal with those moments depends on who we are and what has worked for us in the past. I have employed several tactics over the years, but here are the ones I use the most:
>
> One, I practice more (or better). Sometimes the best way to regain your confidence is from good old-fashioned hard work. Whether it's more swings in the cage, more time analyzing video, or even a more strenuous workout in the gym, I find that making changes (however subtle they may be) gives me the confidence to overcome any sort of slump or mental weakness that I'm experiencing.
>
> Two, I use perspective. Eventually, this technique has diminishing returns, but I often remind myself just how lucky I am to be a professional athlete, to be a husband and father and equipped to handle life after baseball. These thoughts tend to take the pressure off despite their simplicity.

> Three, I'll get mad. Sometimes, when channeled correctly, anger and frustration can be beneficial. The key, of course, is using that added adrenaline and focus in the right way. Baseball isn't like football, where the more adrenaline you have, the better you usually play. So I've tried to learn how to capitalize on the physical benefits of adrenaline while maintaining mental clarity.

I asked him if any of his coaches were especially helpful, and he mentioned how much he appreciated the "incredible stoicism" of Joe Maddon (Tampa Bay, more recently the world champion Chicago Cubs) and Bob Melvin (Oakland): "I've found that the best coaches teach more by their actions than by their words. If I've recently failed but come back to the dugout and get encouragement from a coach (or anything short of negativity for that matter), then I'll feel less fear of failure the next time."

Two Olympians Speak

Lea Maurer has had a storybook career in swimming: Olympic gold medalist, world-record holder in the 400-meter medley relay, American record holder, gold medalist at the 1998 World Championships in the 100-meter backstroke, three-time NCAA champion, coach of the Stanford women's team that won back-to-back PAC 10 championships, and coach of Lake Forest High School's team that won the Illinois State Championship (and the mythical national championship—based on times). She was also the swimming partner and close friend of one of the most decorated US swimmers, Jenny Thompson, who swam at Dover (New Hampshire) High School (I practice at a pool named for her).

I asked her about low points in this great career and she had no problem coming up with some good ones. In her sophomore year in high school, she had a breakthrough swim in the nationals: up to this point she had consistently been out of medal contention, finishing fifth or ninth in big meets. But in this meet she posted the best time in the prelims and was seeded first—her coach John Collins told her this would be her breakthrough swim:

> At this point you could do a backstroke, starting where you could stand and hold the platform. But I couldn't hold my grip on the platform and I fell right on my fanny. And there was a no-false-start rule. You never

> really knew, sometimes they let you get back up, but they didn't and I was disqualified. And I remember going back to the workout on Monday when I returned and I said to him, "How do you keep coaching me when I perpetually disappoint you?"

Collins borrowed a line from a popular cartoon show of that day, *Pinky and the Brain*. In each episode, the Brain, a mutant mouse, develops a plan to take over the world, and in each episode that plan is thwarted by Pinky, his inept partner—and they fail spectacularly. Yet the next episode always starts with Pinky asking the Brain, "What are we going to do today, Brain?" and the Brain calmly answers, "The same thing we do every day. Try to take over the world."

Collins concluded, "My job, regardless of what happened yesterday, is to make you the best in the world." In our interview we returned several times to this capacity to move on, and what it takes to do that.

Maurer's biggest disappointment came in 1996 when she failed to make the US Olympic team, after her great success at the 1992 Olympics. In the interval the Chinese swim team had suddenly (and suspiciously) emerged as a powerhouse, dominating the 1994 World Championships. She and Thompson knew that they had to train *as if* they were on steroids if they had any chance—but Lea missed the team, finishing fifth, and Thompson only made the relay. At this point, her life was also changing—she got married and became an English teacher and high school swimming coach, meaning she could not train full time, a huge impediment to continuing at this level.

Again John Collins was key, encouraging her to return to swimming, to get fit and "rekindle that love of moving in the water. It felt like I was a ballerina—I loved the process, the art of it." In one of swimming's great comebacks she made the US team for the 1998 World Championships and won the 100-meter backstroke in record American time, and she was also part of the winning medley relay. She credits Collins with helping her "get back to basics"—and I asked her what that meant.

> The basics are day-in, day-out. Almost none of the past, good or bad, is going to help you. Come without programmed expectations and focus on the moment at hand and whatever ignites passion and happiness for you. Holding on to that pain haunts you and you don't want anything haunting you. You want to move on and literally have a clean slate as much as possible. Have a trash can and write down whatever is bothering you

and put it in the trash can before workouts. For me, I am a happy swimmer. There are people who are ferocious and angry swimmers. He wanted me to go back to where I am laughing at a meet, closer to the Lea he knew. The basics means: come to the workout with enthusiasm, and enjoy it—come away that you learned something, you shared something, you laughed at something. Those two hours were not going through the motions. You were actively engaged both intellectually and personally.

> It's like when I go to church; I never feel worse after I have gone to church. Swim workouts should be that way. You should come away feeling better at the end of the workout, regardless of whether you missed an interval, or that you didn't feel great. There should be something that you took away from that two-hour or three-hour event in which you were challenged or you grew or you helped someone, so you are growing in some way. That should happen every time you are in a workout.

And writing, she believes, helps.

I knew that Lea had her Stanford swimmers keep journals, and I asked about how this writing helped them learn from their experiences. Like Rich Kent she used them for analyzing races, but she also encouraged her athletes to write down stories they wanted to remember, times when they made a breakthrough in practice, or just funny moments. Here is one of her own favorite stories:

> One of my favorite Jenny stories is about when we were working out really hard. She used to chew gum while she swam, but I don't know how she did that. So she said, "Shoot I dropped my gum." And the next repeat, I dove down in the lane we were in and I picked up and gave her the gum. She popped it in her mouth. And right before she pushed off she said, "That's not my gum." And she is so intense, I had to say three Hail Marys because I thought she was going to rip my jugular out in the next set. And I'm thinking, "Oh God is she going to get sick?" Trying to be so helpful. She and I went to the Olympics together, we were roommates together, we set American records on relays, we set a world record on the medley relay, and that is one of my best Jenny Thompson moments.

Maurer consistently used the word *fictions* to describe some of the demons, unhealthy projections, that interfere with performance. Her concept recalls the term *imagination*, which has not always had the positive connotation it now has. Imagination takes us out of the present, and into projected futures. As such, it

It is not a simple matter of adopting a positive mindset—it is hard work, dependent on coaches, team-mates, parents. It is also dependent on personal and learned strategies for disciplining the mind, when the temptations are so great to leave the present.

is the basis of fear and anxiety—it takes the athlete, in Lea's words, "to the emotional well that can be depleting." It is not hard to imagine this temptation when the stakes are so high, as they surely are at a meet like the Olympic trials. There are coaches and friends and family who might be disappointed with a poor performance—or be forced to unload tickets if you don't qualify. And we are always performing to that most demanding of audiences—ourselves.

At moments like this, with so many possible anxieties, elite athletes must learn to police themselves, to avoid these projections, these fictions—enabling them to relax and focus on realities. It is not a simple matter of adopting a positive mindset—it is hard work, dependent on coaches, teammates, parents. It is also dependent on personal and learned strategies for disciplining the mind, when the temptations are so great to leave the present.

* * * *

Whenever Jennie Marshall showed up at our Masters swimming practices and swam in your lane, you knew you were in for a serious seventy-five minutes. Whatever the workout she would follow it exactly, even if it meant almost no rest between intervals; she would set a demanding pace at the beginning of the workout and maintain it. She has always been for me the model of a serious, committed athlete, even though swimming is not her primary sport. No screwing around.

Jennie's primary sport is rowing. She was a medalist in the World Championships, and a member of the 1988 US Olympic team, and for years a legendary coach in the area. I had always wanted to interview her about her rowing career, and this chapter gave me that opportunity. And she came prepared with the major failure story of her career.

The year was 1987, and Jennie had moved with her partner to Cambridge, Massachusetts so that she could train with an elite group of rowers, under the guidance of the Olympic coach. She actually lived in the Harvard boathouse ("with the mice") and split her time between coaching and training. Jennie had barely missed the 1984 team, had medaled in world competition, and seemed a good possibility for the 1988 team. The first big test, a competition called "speed orders," was held in Princeton. Rows of six would compete, and the top three would go on to the next round, and the process repeated.

> I went to the first speed order and I was just *so slow*. Just so slow. I had changed my whole life to do this, to be on the Olympic team, and on the first big test of my abilities and potential, I was so slow. It was a deep sense of humiliation how slow I was. I think I was pretty much blind with humiliation, deaf with humiliation. All the athletes I coached would know I failed.

As she was putting away her boat in the Harvard boathouse, her coach, realizing how distraught she was, tried to console her: "Jennie, it's OK." And Jennie shot back, "It's not OK."

> It came from my gut. She couldn't say anything to me at that moment that was going to move me to a better place—and I didn't want to go to a better place. I wanted to be in this place until I figured out what to do next to fix it. I didn't rush through the discomfort, and I think that was the message to her. It was like not "just move on"—then it's just talk. I had to feel this long enough to feel it in a true muscle-based way. And it's less about where I finished and more about the shame of not showing up emotionally and physically to the thing I said I wanted to do.
>
> I had to ask myself, what's the truth of the situation? Am I training as hard as I should? So the next step for me is a lot of questions: Why did this happen? And if it was about "not trying," what does trying look like? People say that all the time, "try harder," but what does that really look like? So let's break that down. Is my intensity high enough? Is the volume high enough? Am I taking care of myself between practices? Is nutrition an issue? You move from a deeply emotional place to a pragmatic place through questioning.
>
> So I think there is an intentionality to failure. I'm going to try harder but I know exactly what I am going to do. And I am going to work on this until I see that it works. And there is no guarantee. It's terrifying because you think, what if I take these additional steps, committing to all these things that I say I'll do—and what if you go back and it happens again? And you can't answer

> "After all, you are not going to get anything if you don't get it wrong the first time. Maybe I'm not even going to call it failure, I'm going to call it a 'first try,' to switch the perception from a finite thing to a first try. You have to get something to get somewhere."

that question until you go back. And maybe it happens again and maybe it doesn't. That's the part about being comfortable with being uncomfortable: it's saying, "I don't know if this is going to work, but I am willing to try."

After all, you are not going to get anything if you don't get it wrong the first time. Maybe I'm not even going to call it failure, I'm going to call it a "first try," to switch the perception from a finite thing to a first try. You have to get something to get somewhere. So I don't go back to the next speed orders. I don't try out for the team. I don't feel humiliated. What did I get out of that?

She went on to make the 1988 Olympic squad and compete in the Seoul games in 1988.

Jennie now works as a literacy coach in New Hampshire and I asked her how experiences as coach and athlete have shaped her work with teachers.

> I realized that I learned things about perseverance and being willing to fail—and that's something I see in working with teachers. I remember working with a teacher on a technique for teaching reading—I said something like "What if you tried it? It doesn't have to be perfect. What if you just did it?" And she was so mad at me: "It *does* have to be perfect!" And my question back to her was: "How do you know what you are doing now is perfect?"

Jennie's reaction to her failure at speed orders, and her insistence in using her discomfort, calls to mind a section of a Robert Frost poem, "A Servant to Servants":

> By good rights I ought not to have so much
> Put on me, but there seems no other way.
> Len says one steady pull ought to do it.
> He says the best way out is always through.

For her the only way ahead was to feel the humiliation, not to minimize it or rationalize it or escape it—even if that was a possibility. The "way out is always through" using that emotion to propel a thought process that can be intentional and focused. Perhaps the most famous case of an athlete using embarrassment to his advantage is Michael Jordan's assignment to the JV team in his sophomore year in high school. His resentment and reliving of this moment was rocket fuel throughout his career and beyond.

Learning from Athletes

It is an evolutionary fact that our emotional memories are powerful, even primary—and although analysis and narrative help us process failure, they can't erase entirely emotional memory, what the old show *Wide World of Sports* called "the agony of defeat" (showing, every Saturday, the same ski jumper falling off the side of the launching ramp).

I decided to apply the insights of these coaches and athletes to one of my own acutely embarrassing failures. I am not a regular speaker at national conferences but I do some of it, and recently agreed to do two ninety-minute workshops at a regional reading conference. When I saw the program, the two sessions were early afternoon: 1:00 to 2:30 and late afternoon: 3:00 to 4:30, actually the end of the conference. The first session, attended by over 100 people, went reasonably well, though I expect that the audience wanted more practical help. But I felt drained after it, and not at all ready for the next session, which was on a different topic (actually the subject of my book, *Minds Made for Stories*).

As I waited for the audience to arrive, it didn't. There were about fifteen people in a salon with 150 chairs—attendees were scattered everywhere, and made no attempt to come forward or even sit with another person. I'm sure they felt trapped in a session nobody wanted to attend. I knew immediately that what I planned, and extensive PowerPoint, would not work. And I thought my best shot would be to try to make it more a workshop with some writing prompts—so I asked them to come forward and form a group—which they did *very reluctantly*. I used part of my PowerPoint to introduce my topic, and then we moved awkwardly to the prompts, which they tried *very reluctantly*, and were resistant to sharing. Perhaps they knew I was winging it.

By this point, about forty-five minutes into the presentation, I was out of strategies. I don't believe I can convey to you the negative energy in that room. We were *all* trapped. So I said that because it was late in the day, I would sum up some points and allow them to leave. I showed the end of my PowerPoint, thanked them for coming, sent them on their way, and felt absolutely terrible. I felt it physically, in my gut, in the back of my knees. Here I had come halfway across the country, was paid well for the afternoon, and I was dismissing class early. I felt like I had cheated the reading association that had contracted with me to present.

If I view this failure microscopically, I take away two lessons. One: avoid giving back to back sessions like this late in the day. Some presenters thrive on this kind of schedule; I don't. And two: it was bad luck. My presentation wasn't right for the conference and particularly for this time slot. Maybe nothing would have worked, certainly nothing in my repertoire at the time.

But as much as I can explain this failure, some pain and embarrassment persists. I can't analyze it away, not completely. It is not debilitating, or evidence that I can't be a good presenter. But it is there. And I have to accept it as part of the package of being a presenter, a teacher, a human being, being me.

Yet listening to these great athletes and coaches convinces me that we have psychological and social resources that can help us move on and not be, in Lea Maurer's words, "haunted" by these memories. She calls these memories "fictions," not because they didn't happen, but because they are not helpful—and what matters is the work before us, the basics, this practice, this set of swimming intervals, and if we gain something by our efforts, cross some threshold, we put that past behind us. It's about the process, the moment, bracketing out the past, and even the future—it is being there. Her motto is "reset, reset, reset."

And even if we cannot totally bracket these feelings, we can use them, and give ourselves credit that part of feeling bad about a session like this was my deep desire to do it well. It is the inverse of a positive trait.

I can also ask myself what practically I can do to be better in these situations, perhaps watching carefully the best presenters at these conferences. I can get a better plan B. I can become pragmatic. What can I control?

Draw the damn circle. "Next shot, next shot."

CHAPTER 10

What Is This About?

> *Our errors are surely not such awfully solemn things.*
>
> —WILLIAM JAMES, "THE WILL TO BELIEVE"

Early in my career at the University of New Hampshire, I would be working on an essay or chapter, and I would give my neighbor Don Murray a call to ask if he would read it and give me advice on how to improve it. Invariably, no matter the time of day, he would say, "Come on over." So I'd go across Mill Pond Road, up his driveway, in the side door where his wife Minnie Mae would show me some miraculous amaryllis she was tending. Then I'd weave my way through their cluttered basement past shelves of canned fruit, gathering layers of dust, to his study where he would be listening to Bach cantatas.

Figure 10-1

I would sometimes startle him out of eighteenth-century Saxony and hand him my writing. Even as an older man, Don was big—around six feet three inches, maybe 260 pounds (Figure 10-1). And he would stand as he read, with his glasses pulled up on his forehead and the text just inches from his face. He read quickly, flipping pages every few seconds, it seemed, and then he would always ask me the same question: "What is this about?"

At first this sort of pissed me off. "What is this about?" Doesn't it have a title, and a clear topic? But I would begin to answer, and I'd find myself fumbling and taking several restarts to answer his question. Then he might say, "If that is what it's about, you don't really get there until about page 5."

It was a great lesson, and I still can hear his voice in my head. And it is a fair question about this book. The concept of embarrassment, to use Henry James' words, "stops nowhere." It invades all subjects, applies to teachers and students, to all of us. It is inextricably linked to some of our most powerful and debilitating feelings: shame, fear, regret, caution, and avoidance. Entire research fields have evolved to study these "self-conscious" emotions—and entire sections of bookstores offer advice on how to deal them. I have often felt like a thief as I traversed these fields, stealing here and there, hoping that I was doing that ethically, if there can be an ethical theft, a principled home invasion.

In this final chapter I want to answer Don's question, and revisit themes that stitch together the wide range of topics in this book.

The Performance of Self. There is great appeal to think of ourselves as possessing an authentic, presocial self—perhaps located somewhere in the upper part of our bodies. "To thine own self be true," Polonius advises Laertes, "And it must follow, as the night the day Thou canst not then be false to any man." This advice wasn't a great help to him, as he was pulled between so many roles—son, lover, avenger, student, prince. Erving Goffman challenges this conception: our sense of self comes from our capacity to take on, often effortlessly, any number of social roles. He reminds us that the word *person* comes from a root word for "mask"—we are, whether we are aware of it or not, always on stage.

Shy people know this. They (and I include myself in this group) are always aware of the demands of being in public, feeling judged, experiencing concern about entering into conversations and sustaining them—and always envious of those who seem to do this naturally. As Susan Cain points out in her book, *Quiet* (2012), we often seek solitude at the end of a day when we are constantly with people: we choose not to go out to dinner with the crowd, and we want to feel the relief of nonperformance.

If social behavior is performance, there are risks involved, social pain involved. If we fail to measure up to expected standards, if we reveal what Goffman (1959) calls "discrepant" information, we lose face. And if we consider situations where we are learning a new skill, this learning almost inevitably involves some public awkwardness. If a student raises his hand to answer a question, and does so incorrectly (and is told so), that public display causes social pain—embarrassment, regret, shame, loss of social standing, performative anxiety about taking such a risk in the future. Social psychologists go to great lengths to distinguish these self-conscious emotions, but all of them, it seems to me, flow from a deeply human need to perform competently in public.

Gains and Losses. Although all of these emotions can be painful, sometimes acutely so, they serve an important social function of regulating behavior, of sanctioning violations of social norms. Expressions of embarrassment and shame work to reintegrate the individual back into good standing—this may be the social function of the blush. I have colleagues who also swear that the possibility of an embarrassing public failure motivates them to perform. The fact that embarrassment is a universal phenomenon, among humans and primates, is evidence of the profoundly important evolutionary role it plays. Societies cannot exist without norms—and without psychological sanctions for transgressing those norms. To be "shameless" is to be dangerously deviant. We wouldn't want it any other way.

If we were really good at assessing the social damage of our missteps, all of these emotions would be useful correctives. But we're not. There are other inherent biases that interfere with an accurate perception of consequences. One tendency is loss aversion—a bias toward experiencing the pain of loss more than the gratification of gain. Behavioral economists have shown that investors regularly make irrational decisions when they fail to take a reasonable risk for fear of experiencing a loss. I would argue the same principle applies to the "loss of face." There is a risk in being singled out in a class for attention—you might fumble, be wrong, be exposed—and often you can protect that status by being silent, looking attentive. For some students—for example, girls in a math class—that calculation might be different because they labor under a stereotype, so that any difficulty they might expose could be seen as evidence that they don't belong.

Whenever I hear that "learning is natural for young children and schools kill that spontaneity," I feel that we ignore the challenge of self-consciousness. For the self-conscious student, the *natural* bias is often toward caution, not exposing one's awkwardness and error in a learning situation. The complex task of teaching is to structure the risk/reward equation so that we minimize what might be lost by being awkward and approximate. Almost all of the teaching strategies in this book try to do that.

Distortion. Humans (and perhaps primates) are distinct from other animals in their capacity to be "self-conscious"—to be able to look at themselves, and judge themselves, from the standpoint of Another. As noted previously, this capacity serves an evolutionary survival function of policing human behavior and limiting deviance. In his famous encounter with Joseph McCarthy, the brilliant attorney Joseph Welsh finally confronted him with the question: "Have you no sense of decency?" In other words, have you lost the capacity to apply basic standards of behavior to yourself, to see yourself in the proper way? If, so, you are a truly lost soul.

But this process of internalizing the perspective, the "gaze" of Another, often produces unwarranted shame, embarrassment, even self-loathing. If a race or class or gender or physical feature is perceived as inferior, there is a danger that prejudice is internalized. The member of any discriminated group then bears a double burden: the overt restrictions placed on the group, and the more poisonous self-perception shaped by this prejudice. Toni Morrison portrays this internalization in *The Bluest Eye*: the main character Pecola Breedlove is ashamed of her black skin and curly hair—and prays for the blue eyes and blond hair that will allow her to be loved. The first great heroine of American literature, Hester Prynne in *The Scarlet Letter* (Hawthorne), refuses to internalize—or accept—the judgment of her society. Her lack of shame is more threatening to those around her than her original act of adultery. Our capacity for self-awareness is not an unmixed gift, because it opens the way for stigma and stereotyping—the social pain they bring, and the educational challenge of combating them.

Even those of us who are not in stigmatized or negatively stereotyped groups can judge ourselves too harshly because we measure ourselves against unrealistic, idealized standards.

Imagine a gloomy day in early December. I am teaching a late afternoon class. Night has already begun to fall—and I don't want to be there. Not that I dislike teaching this class, but on this day, I feel tired and would so much rather stay home and catch up on *The New Yorker*. I may share this feeling with my wife at home—because I am in Goffman's terms "backstage" there. But as I walk into my classroom in Hamilton Smith Hall, I do not share this information. I put on my game face, summon up what optimism I can muster, and launch in. I try to live up to an idealized image of what a teacher should be.

Let's say this was a class of future English teachers, and for the sake of argument let's say I am successful that day—and because I didn't disclose my feelings, students can assume *the performance is who I am*—confident, committed, upbeat, prepared, even funny. In the future they might even measure themselves against me as if I am some kind of role model. But *they* experience their own discrepant feelings of insecurity, frustration, fatigue, failure—and feel they are the outlier or imposter because they imagine, falsely, that I (or other teachers they look up to) didn't have these same feelings. They never knew that before every class I taught in my college career, I paced the floor of my office, trying to keep my anxiety in check—but students would write on their evaluation that I am "laid back." If they only knew.

Idealization has its uses, providing something to aspire to. But I agree with George Orwell: "Saints should always be judged guilty until they are proved innocent" (1998, 1349). If we measure ourselves against unrealizable models, for example, the superteachers we read about in books, we are setting ourselves up for failure. The successes in teaching will seem so intermittent and impermanent by comparison. Do these teachers have that disruptive boy who takes so much attention? Does she feel as drained at the end of the day? An observer might be more generous and point out successes in our teaching, innovations they might steal. But the door stays closed because we feel we don't measure up to a model, which may, after all, be a fiction. We don't want to be revealed.

Another source of distortion is what psychologists call the "spotlight effect"—the illusion that we are as visible to others as we are to ourselves. In another era it would be called "vanity." A teenage girl at the lunch counter hesitates to take more than a salad, for fear of appearing to be an overeater—when no one in the lunch room is watching or judging her so severely. Or a time I have already recounted: I struggle in a late afternoon workshop and revisit it painfully two years later. But realistically, for participants it probably blended into their conference experience, barely remembered if recalled at all, and not remotely equivalent to my memory.

This misconception might, in Shelly Taylor's words, be called a "positive illusion"—it is useful to take ourselves seriously, to care deeply about our actions even if others are not affected as much as we imagine. But this tendency is also a source of unnecessary pain and distortion; we mentally punish ourselves for crimes when we have only committed mishaps. We overestimate the severity of this judging audience when our actual audience, if we even have one, is not as focused on us—and even if they do observe us they are likely to be more tolerant (or forgetful) than the audience we construct in our heads.

Voices in the Head

In his essay "Teaching the Other Self," Don Murray describes the act of writing this way:

> The act of writing might be described as a conversation between two workmen muttering to each other on the workbench. The self speaks, the other self listens and responds. The self proposes, the other self considers. The two selves collaborate: a problem is spotted, discussed, defined; solutions are proposed, rejected, suggested, attempted, tested, discarded, accepted. (2009, 87–88)

This is the cooperative, benign "other self" that we would all want to have. But there is no guarantee that the voices are constructive ones. It might be a voice that embodies social prejudices or severe critics or abusing parents. It might be a voice like the one Pecola Breedlove heard, that told her she would be loved if she only had blue eyes. Or, we might hear consistently cautionary voices—"Don't stand out. Play it safe. Why risk losing what you have?" It is probably the voice Mike Rose's student heard when he proclaimed, "I just want to be average."

Murray's position is a version of a broader claim by the great sociologist George Herbert Mead, who claimed that selfhood—being a self—was possible because we take perspectives on ourselves. We can internalize a "generalized other" that we are in dialogue with (2015). We can be both subject and object, actor and audience. We construct that "generalized other" from our social interactions with peers, parents, teachers, coaches—and there is no guarantee that this "generalized other" will be the collaborative partner, the sidekick, Murray describes. To put it another way, if students are to take on a growth mindset, they need to engage in the kind of internal dialogue that allows for an acceptance of failure and risk-taking. And as I have argued, there are powerful evolutionary biases that distort perception and work against this open, fluid, undefensive sense of self. As parents and teachers we have work to do to help these inner conversations be productive ones.

Language Matters. One of the truly great professional books of my generation is Peter Johnston's *Choice Words* (2014). It is difficult to finish that short book unchanged. Like most transformative books, it takes as its topic something we are loosely aware of—the way we talk to students—and brings it into absolute focus. It is more than a guide to how we might participate in classroom talk: I believe it lays out an architecture for how a mind can work, how a real learner thinks. As this talk is internalized, as it becomes part of our own inner dialogue, our own self-questioning, it liberates us from the dichotomous world of right and wrong (the source of so much shame)—and shows the way to explore options, ask questions, test possibilities, explain thinking—to be agents, heroes of our own learning stories.

As I reread Johnston's book, I recalled a research project I conducted early in my career that involved recording numerous group book discussions of first graders, led by a master teacher, Pat McLure. Sometimes these kids made predictions so outlandish, judgments so bizarre (you know, ducks that would take over the world), I had to suppress a smile, and I watched Pat lean in and say, "Hmm. Why do you think that?" And there *would* be a logical route to that answer. The more outlandish the observation, the more interested she became.

The focus in her class, as it was with the shape problems in the math chapter, was not on correctness but on justification. With Johnston's disarmingly simple prompts ("Why do you think that?" "How else can we look at this?" "Who has another . . . ?" "What if . . . ?"), we are inviting students to imagine a more complex (and hopefully tolerant) world of multiple perspectives.

What if . . . ? For example, what if we turned that map at the front of the class upside down—so South America is on top and we are below the equator—it feels, well, disorienting, even diminishing. We realize our bias favoring that which is above, as if we are viewing a human body. There are cultural weights to the "top" and "bottom." But viewed from outer space, isn't this upside down view just as justified?

You Need a Coach. In the PBS film *Raising Cain* (2006), psychologist Michael Thompson is interviewing a group of teenage boys from Chelsea, Massachusetts. He asks them to name the most important man in their lives. One of them answers, "I am." At first, it seems an egotistical answer, but as the film follows this young man through his day, we realize he is simply being accurate. There is no man to be a model, to offer advice, or set limits. In his book *Our Kids* (2016), Robert Putnam argues that one form that privilege takes is in the "thick" network of adults that can be part of children's lives—parents, relatives, friends of the family, teachers, coaches. Putnam singles out that extracurricular activities are so important in helping less privileged kids construct that network, where they learn crucial skills in teamwork, coping with failure, learning new skills.

In my own school district we have a virtual army of volunteer coaches, including Paul Kerrigan, who instructs eight- and nine-year-olds at the level where they must hit pitched baseballs. It's very frightening for many of them, and not swinging and walking is a tempting choice. Only it doesn't teach you how to hit—you have to stand in and swing the bat. So Kerrigan talked to his team about needing to swing and even strike out; he would praise them for "good strikeouts," where they didn't back off and swung at good pitches, maybe even fouled off a pitch. In effect, he framed failure as success, or an approximation of success.

Coaches can also help keep the focus forward. Logically, once a game is over or a test completed, the results cannot be undone, but most of us have a natural tendency to relive those events, maybe reexperience the pain, when we need to move on, take whatever lessons we can from the loss but move on. Olympian and former world-record holder Lea Maurer tells this story of her coach taking her out to TGI Fridays after a painful loss:

> I lost to my archrival in a fairly big meet before nationals. My coach brought me to TGI Fridays and it's fair to say in general swim coaches and swim coaches of women, they want you to be lean, you know pound to power ratios so desserts are limited most of the time—and he orders Death by Chocolate, chocolate cake covered by chocolate, and he goes, "We are going to eat this, mourn the loss, and never speak of it again."

So you move on.

Draw the Damn Circle. Because we have a predisposition to distortion, we need coaches (and I use the term broadly to mean advice givers) to help us work through difficulty and provide models that we might use to self-advise. Most of our activity, necessarily, is guided by habit and routine—what William James called an "effortless custodian." When these routines fail us, we sense that difficulty emotionally—as annoyance, frustration, disappointment, anger, even, if difficulty persists, as embarrassment and shame. I don't believe there is any way to avoid the emotionality of failed routines; in fact, the sensation of failure is often a spur to real thinking.

But to use failure productively we need to perform an act of translation. We cannot continue to deal with ourselves in global attitudes. With the help of a patient listener, we must move from this overheated emotional realm to an analytic stance. My embarrassing failure in my first cross-country meet was not due to a deep character flaw, or not wanting to win enough, or not being able to work through the pain of distance running. It was not some big, disqualifying problem. If I had been able to process it (translate it) with my coach, we might have come to a less self-condemning conclusion about pacing or warming up. And we might have come up with some practice strategies like experimenting with different paces for the first quarter mile of the race.

This is a version of "drawing the damn circle." What can I change? What can't I change? The race is over. My dropping out cannot be undone. But if I can be shown a way to look at it microscopically, break it apart, I can find a way forward. This is what Rich Kent called being a "student of the game." With the help of a coach, I can set a workable task that can help me solve my problem; together we can draw the circle and frame tasks to put inside it. This process is not simply a better way to train for cross-country, it prevents pointless self-condemnation and disappointment—or possibly the impulsive action of quitting altogether.

Thresholds. Janet Emig is one of the pioneers in writing research, and in her distinguished career she worked extensively with teachers. Here is how she often began her summer writing classes: teachers would come into the classroom to see her working at a desk, journal open, writing. She didn't look up as they entered, but on the board she had written, "I am writing. Please join me."

Emig created an inviting and simple entry point. Details could follow, but the opening to the act of writing was uncluttered. No rubrics, no terminology, no explaining of assignments—simply the invitation to write. This concept of thresholds is central to this book and makes me think how much care goes into doorways in architecture, evidence of the psychological importance of entering. I also think of my early experiences in my dad's biology lab when he would put a slide of a cell membrane under the microscope and ask me, "Well, what do you see?"

In physics, one of the few principles that I retain is "bodies at rest tend to stay at rest, and bodies in motion tend to stay in motion"—or something like that. There are huge temptations to "stay at rest," refrigerators to raid, websites to check. We can be daunted by the task of writing a paper, solving a complex math problem, interpreting a difficult poem. We can feel stupid and inadequate, clueless about how to begin.

We can lower the threshold in writing by practices like freewriting where there is little or no consideration of an audience, where judgment is withheld, where our focus is solely on our thinking that evolves as we write—as we race ahead of the censor and critic. We can lower it in reading and interpretation, by asking students to *notice*, to mark the text, and in doing so to assign significance—then to follow the thread of our thinking about that mark. It might be something as simple as picking a word in a poem that seems powerful and meaningful, or creating an alternative title for an essay or poem. The key is to get in motion.

The processes of mathematical thinking were less familiar to me, but I was gratified to see the similarities—often beginning with observations, questions, intuitions, guesses, and importantly, visualization (not coincidentally a primary comprehension strategy in reading comprehension). Stanford professor Jo Boaler, for example, shows how the multiplication problem 18 × 5 can be visualized as a variety of rectangles. We can of course make one that is 18 × 5, but we have two rectangles of 9 × 5, or one rectangle of 10 × 5 and one that is 8 × 5—and so on. We can build number sense by encouraging students to visualize this problem in many possible ways. All of this seems so much more inviting to someone taught under the regimen of right and wrong.

Rigor Is Not the Answer. It is fashionable these days to see "rigor" and "grit" and "stamina" as the key characteristics of a strong learner. We hear again and again of those amazing kids who could wait to eat the marshmallows—and then go on to become the bosses of those who did. The only good kind of gratification, it seems, is delayed gratification.

I will admit that there are clearly times when we have to summon willpower to do something uninteresting but necessary. However, our primary attitude toward any kind of work cannot be, should not be, one of clenched tightness, or anxiety, or even conscious effort. Athletes, as they get ready to perform, loosen up—they don't "tighten up." I have always found that the state of mind I seek is one of calm, of receptiveness, of playfulness, of an open time horizon—and the rituals I employ, particularly the music I listen to, work to get me into that state.

The great psychologist William James makes an illuminating distinction about attention. He claims that we can attend voluntarily (through an act of will) or involuntarily. If, for example, you are aware of having to push yourself to read these last few pages, if you are wondering how all this fits—or pausing to gather energy to finish—you are giving my words voluntary attention. If, on the other hand, you are moving along with me as you would in a good conversation, not conscious of expending effort, you are attending involuntarily. According to James,

> There's a common notion that self-discipline is a freakish peculiarity of writers—that writers differ from other people by possessing enormous and equal portions of talent and willpower. They grit their powerful teeth and go into their little rooms. I think that's a bad misunderstanding of what impels the writer. What impels the writer is a deep love and respect for language, for literary forms, for books. It's a privilege to muck about in sentences all morning. It's a challenge to bring off a powerful effect, or to tell the truth about something. You don't do it from willpower; you do it from an abiding passion for the field. I'm sure it's the same in every other field.
>
> Annie Dillard, "To Fashion a Text"

"involuntary intellectual attention is immediate when we follow in thought a train of images exciting or interesting per se" (1985, 90).

Voluntary attention cannot be sustained for long periods of time—it works more in spurts, and often with the purpose of helping us reenter a state of unconscious engagement. If we are listening to a complex lecture, we might periodically become aware that we are daydreaming and push ourselves to get back in the flow of the talk, to enter what James calls a state in which we are not aware of paying attention. In fact the concept of "flow" developed by Mihaly Csikszentmihalyi, delineates a state of engagement that seems to unfold with effortful direction.

The quality of genius, according to James, comes not from some superhuman capacity for grit, but from a capacity to follow a stream of thought in which "subjects bud and sprout and grow." We cannot sustain involuntary attention if the object of our attention is unchanging, or we cease to see it as changing. It becomes dead and uninviting. But the "genius" can keep the idea moving. James concludes that "it is their genius making them attentive, not their attention making geniuses of them" (94). Or put another way, the qualities of persistence that we can call "grit" or "stamina" are really by-products (or perhaps the outer appearance) of a capacity for sustained engagement, for keeping things in motion. If we make grit the goal, we are telling the wrong story.

And even if we don't claim to be a genius, we become more effective thinkers if we can keep an object of attention alive and moving. We don't stop with the first impression; we don't give up when we meet difficulty. We can ask questions, make associations, explore alternatives, name our confusion, ask how we can resolve it. We can learn to sustain, in John Dewey's terms, "an attitude of suspended conclusion" (1910).

Toward Self-Generosity

I realize that many of the suggestions I have made throughout this book are consistent with the current emphasis on adopting a "growth mindset." If there is a difference, it is one of emphasis, because there are formidable obstacles to achieving this openness of self, this capacity to embrace failure and free ourselves from fixed and limiting identities. What is sometimes missing from these discussions is *struggle*. Evolutionary and social forces (prejudices/stereotypes/stigmas) work against us. Our own vanity and fear of exposure work against us. Our innate predisposition to experience losses more acutely than gains work against us. The idealized models we aspire to can work against us—prompting us to doubt our competence and shrink from being observed. To learn something new, we must be publicly awkward, and there is nothing "natural" about wanting to be revealed this way. Anxiety is our lot as humans, as learners, and it takes a complex range of supports to deal with it.

To learn something new, we must be publicly awkward, and there is nothing "natural" about wanting to be revealed this way. Anxiety is our lot as humans, as learners, and it takes a complex range of supports to deal with it.

We may need to adopt a growth mindset about achieving a growth mindset. It is not a matter of "adopting" something. We are talking about a lifelong struggle, and the humbling responsibility of parent and teachers to embolden students (and ourselves) to take public risks—which means we need to be models, and show what it means to speak out.

A couple of years ago I was flattered to have received the Badass Teacher (BAT) Award from my fellow troublemakers in New Hampshire. I wear with pride the T-shirt with the image of a bat on it.

But truth be told, I am not a badass. If I were to categorize myself as a courageous or fearful person, the balance would be toward fearful, even on minor decisions (Should I have my ice cream in a cup or a cone on this hot day? Damn!).

Anxiety pervades my own emotional life—it has been the bottomless well I could dip into as I wrote this book.

But here I am speaking up—about talking back. I have been thinking about that a lot in the current climate of top-down education reform. When we speak out, we disrupt a seeming consensus—an expectation that we are in agreement, on the same team, even on the same page. After all the experts have spoken, the authorities are lined up. The Common Core is so *common*, what's the point?

Sometimes we may fear retribution, but usually the discomfort is enough to shut us down. To speak up violates a desire that I think we all have to be cooperative human beings, to perform in an agreed-upon way and avoid embarrassment. There is a real seduction in following the rules, going with the consensus (even an artificial one)—it eases stress both for us and for others in the room. I know that I feel it.

When we speak up, when we challenge the expected consensus, when we question the mandate coming down, we create discomfort for everyone—for ourselves, surely, but for others in the room. They will notice the small strain in your voice. There will often be an awkward silence afterward as if we had made some inappropriate bodily noise. And after speaking you may (if you are like me) question whether it was the right thing to do and berate yourself for not making your point well enough. For some, this speaking up may be unstressful, but I suspect that for most of us it's hard.

I have always felt this discomfort acutely and worked instinctively to avoid public discord. Only recently have I located one possible source. I was blessed with a great father to whom I owe so much. But he was a drinker, and undeniably (though I long denied it) an alcoholic. This meant that I never knew when I would set him off, when some inadvertent act I couldn't control, like opening my mouth when I chewed my food, would bring down criticism and anger. I developed a sense of being hyperalert to any sign of possible anger and would avoid—if I could—any precipitating action, with him or anyone else. I came to believe that nothing good came from public discord and disagreement, from anyone being upset, from anger.

I can't say that this alertness and caution have been totally bad things. People with tempers, prone to angry displays, who "don't hold back," can be damaging. Things said in anger cannot be unsaid. But this caution can be inhibiting. When I speak up, when I say, "I think it will be a mistake if we go in this direction," I've come to realize that people in the room probably won't think I'm a bad person, though possibly an annoying one. And if they do—that is their problem. In fact, dissent may open up space for others. I often don't carry the day, but I have come to feel better in the long run. The more I speak up, the easier it has become, though I feel it in my stomach and voice almost every time.

It calls to mind an observation by Eleanor Roosevelt that I have taken to heart:

> Courage is more exhilarating than fear and in the long run it is easier. We do not have to become heroes overnight, just a step at a time, meeting each thing as it comes, seeing it's not as dreadful as it appeared, discovering we have the strength to stare it down. (1960, 41)

I cannot say I have weathered my own childhood—who has? Anxiety still pervades my worldview. I often operate by imagining the worst possible outcome. But I have come to believe, in my early old age, that we can disentangle ourselves from the fears we carry, and speak our minds.

* * * *

So what can we do? What is this about? Can I make one last try? Maybe "self-generosity" is the best I can come up with. There are blows we cannot avoid, separations and losses we must endure. But we can learn to avoid self-inflicted wounds, needless and unproductive emotional distress that comes from an inevitably distorted view of ourselves—our overrating of the consequences of what we do. We can learn to be kind to ourselves, though we will regularly need the perspective of others to do it. As my brother is fond of saying, we all need a team—to give us perspective and help us drain setbacks of their emotionality so that we can plan a next step. We all need help, and there should be no stigma in seeking it—we must also recognize that seeking help is also a performance that requires social awareness, even training and encouragement to seek it out. It is also a gift we give.

As I imagine it, self-generosity is not some feel-good way of dexterously patting ourselves on the back—of being comfortable and complacent. It is dynamic, productive, creative—connected etymologically with "generative" and "generation." I imagine it as a capacity to keep going in the face of difficulty, a voice that may, for example, remind us that we have met this same difficulty before—or convince us that we have time for another try at something that is hard—or that we need to step back, relax, take a walk, and come back refreshed. In the face of disappointment it can be the voice of champion swimmer Lea Maurer—"Reset, reset, reset." Move on.

If we are lucky, we can internalize voices that can set us right, that can help us recognize what we are doing well, that can keep us from vacillating between exaggerated vanity and exaggerated self-disgust, that can help up break down big challenges into small ones. When I think of these voices, it is not simply or even primarily what they say but the way they say it—the kindness in them.

I have been one of those lucky ones, and as I think of those voices I hear, Don Murray, of course, comes to mind, my meetings with him in that basement office, his asking me what my writing was about. Or when he would look at the title page and say, "Tom, that's not a title, that's a label." All great writing lessons.

But as I think about it, what I best recall is not any specific thing he said—it was the way he looked at me—as if he could see something I couldn't see. He took me seriously at a time when I didn't feel confident to take myself seriously, and he had confidence in me (on the basis of what?). He taught me to trust myself, and to trust that if I paid attention to the words appearing on the page, they could lead the way.

REFERENCES

Ambrose, Steven. 1997. *Undaunted Courage: Meriwether Lewis, Thomas Jefferson, and the Opening of the American West*. New York: Scribner's.

Ashcraft, Mark H., and Elizabeth P. Kirk. 2001. "The Relationships Among Working Memory, Math Anxiety, and Performance." *Journal of Experimental Psychology* 130 (2): 224–37.

Atwell, Nancie. 2007. *The Reading Zone: How to Help Kids Become Skilled, Passionate, Habitual, Critical Readers*. New York: Scholastic.

Bakewell, Sarah. 2016. *At the Existentialist Café: Freedom, Being, and Apricot Cocktails with Jean-Paul Sartre, Simone de Beauvoir, Albert Camus, Martin Heidegger, Maurice Merleau-Ponty and Others*. New York: Other Press.

de Beauvoir, Simone. 1989. *The Second Sex*. New York: Vintage.

Bernstein, Basil. 1970. "A Sociological Approach to Socialization: With References to Educability." In *Language and Poverty*, edited by Frederick Williams, 24–61. London: Academic Press.

Bernstein, Jeremy. 1981. "Profiles: Marvin Minsky." *The New Yorker* (December 14).

Birkerts, Sven. 1994. *The Gutenberg Elegies: The Fate of Reading in an Electronic Age*. New York: Fawcett.

Boaler, Jo. "What Is Number Sense?" www.youcubed.org/what-is-number-sense/. Last accessed May 11, 2017.

Bolles, Edmund. B. 1988. *Remembering and Forgetting: Inquiries into the Nature of Memory*. New York: Walker and Company.

Brandt, Deborah. 2015. *The Rise of Writing: Redefining Mass Literacy*. Cambridge, England: Cambridge University Press.

Brown, Brené. 2010. *The Gifts of Imperfection*. Center City, MN: Hazelden.

Bryson, Bill. 1999. *I'm a Stranger Here Myself: Notes on Returning to America After Twenty Years Away*. New York: Broadway.

Cain, Susan. 2012. *Quiet. The Power of Introverts in a World That Can't Stop Talking*. New York: Broadway Books.

Carnevale, Anthony P., and Donna M. Desrochers. 2003. "The Democratization of Mathematics." In *Quantitative Literacy: Why Numeracy Matters for Schools and Colleges*, 21–30. Princeton, NJ: National Council on Education and the Disciplines.

Castelfranchi, Cristiano, and Isabella Poggi. 1990. "Blushing as a Discourse: Was Darwin Wrong?" In *Shyness and Embarrassment: Perspectives from Social Psychology,* edited by W. Ray Crozier, 230–51. Cambridge, England: Cambridge University Press.

Charon, Rita. 2006. *Narrative Medicine: Honoring the Stories of Illness.* New York: Oxford.

Cohen, Randy. 2010. "Replacement Costs." The Ethicist column. *New York Times Magazine* (January 8): MM, 22. http://www.nytimes.com/2010/01/10/magazine/10FOB-ethicist-t.html?_r=0. Last accessed May 11, 2017.

Coleman, David, and Susan Pimentel. 2012. "Revised Publishers' Criteria for the Common Core State Standards in English Language Arts and Literacy, Grades 3–12." www.corestandards.org/assets/Publishers_Criteria_for_3-12.pdf. Last accessed May 11, 2017.

Coletta, Morrow. 1979. *My Pet Dick.* Pensacola, FL: Beka Books.

Copeland, Charles T., and Henry M. Rideout. 1901. *Freshman English and Theme-Correcting in Harvard College.* New York: Silver, Burdett.

Danielson, Christopher. 2016. *Which One* ***Doesn't*** *Belong?* Portland, ME: Stenhouse.

Dante. 2003. *Dante's Inferno.* Translated by Henry Wadsworth Longfellow. New York: Modern Library.

Dewey, John. 1910. *How We Think.* Boston: D.C. Heath.

Dillard, Annie. 1998. "To Fashion a Text." In *Inventing the Truth: The Art and Craft of Memoir,* edited by William Zinsser. New York: Mariner.

Dostoevsky, Fyodor. 1942. *The Idiot.* Translated by Constance Garnett. New York: Modern Library.

———. 1968. "Notes from the Underground." In *Three Short Novels of Dostoevsky,* translated by Constance Garnett. New York: International Collectors Library.

Dweck, Carol S. 2008. *Mindset: The New Psychology of Success.* New York: Ballantine.

———. 2015. "Carol Dweck Revisits the 'Growth Mindset.'" *Education Week* (September 22). www.edweek.org/ew/articles/2015/09/23/carol-dweck-revisits-the-growth-mindset.html. Last accessed May 11, 2017.

Dyson, Anne Haas. 2016. *Negotiating a Permeable Curriculum: On Literacy, Diversity, and the Interplay of Children's and Teachers' Worlds.* New York: Garn Press.

Elbow, Peter. 1993. "Ranking, Evaluating, and Liking: Sorting Out Three Forms of Judgment." *College English* 55 (2): 187–206.

Egan, Jennifer. 2011. *A Visit from the Goon Squad*. New York: Anchor.

Emerson, Ralph W. 2003. *Nature and Selected Essays*. New York: Penguin.

Eysenck, Michael L., and Manuel G. Calvo. 1992. "Anxiety and Performance: The Processing Efficiency Theory." *Cognition and Emotion* 6 (6): 409–34.

Fallon, Mary M. 1990. "What About Arthur?" In *To Compose: Teaching Writing in High School and College*, edited by Thomas Newkirk. Portsmouth, NH: Heinemann.

Fitzgerald, F. Scott. 1995. *The Great Gatsby*. New York: Scribners.

Flower, Linda. 1990. "Writer-Based Prose: A Cognitive Basis for Problems in Writing." In *To Compose: Teaching Writing in High School and College*, 2nd ed., edited by Thomas Newkirk. Portsmouth, NH: Heinemann.

Frost, Robert. 1917. "A Servant to Servants." In *North of Boston*. Henry Holt: New York.

Gawande, Atul. 2011. "Personal Best: Top Athletes and Singers Have Coaches. Should You?" *The New Yorker* (October 3). www.newyorker.com/magazine/2011/10/03/personal-best. Last accessed May 11, 2017.

Gee, James. 2014. *How to Do Discourse Analysis: A Toolkit*, 2nd ed. London: Routledge.

Gladwell, Malcolm. 2008. *Outliers: The Story of Success*. New York: Little Brown.

Goffman, Erving. 1959. *The Presentation of Self in Everyday Life*. New York: Anchor.

———. 1963. *Stigma: Notes on the Management of Spoiled Identity*. New York: Touchstone.

Grant, Adam. 2016. "Why We Should Stop Grading Students on a Curve." *New York Times* (September 11): SR, 3.

Groopman, Jerome. 2007. *How Doctors Think*. Boston: Houghton Mifflin.

Hacker, Andrew. 2016. *The Math Myth: And Other STEM Delusions*. New York: The New Press.

Harp, Shannon F., and Richard E. Mayer. 1998. "How Seductive Details Do Their Damage: A Theory of Cognitive Interest in Science Learning." *Journal of Educational Psychology* 90 (3): 414–34.

Harris, Christine. 2006. "Embarrassment: A Form of Social Pain." *American Scientist* 94 (6): 524–33.

Hawthorne, Nathaniel. 2002. *The Scarlet Letter*. New York: Penguin.

Horner, Bruce. 2000. "Politics, Pedagogy, and the Profession of Composition: Confronting Commodification and the Contingencies of Power." *Journal of Advanced Composition* 20 (1): 121–53. http://jaconlinejournal.com/archives/vol20.1/horner-politics.pdf. Last accessed May 11, 2017.

How Green Was My Valley. Movie Script. www.springfieldspringfield.co.uk/movie_script.php?movie=how-green-was-my-valley. Last accessed May 11, 2017.

Jack, Anthony Abraham. 2015. "What the Privileged Poor Can Teach Us." *New York Times* (September 13): SR, 12.

James, William. 1985. *Psychology: The Briefer Course*. Notre Dame, Indiana: University of Notre Dame Press.

Jaworski, Adam, and Dafydd Stephens. 1998. "Self-Reports on Silence as a Face-Saving Strategy by People with Hearing Impairment." *International Journal of Applied Linguistics* 8 (1): 61–80.

———. 2000. "The Will to Believe." In *Pragmatism and Other Writings*. New York: Penguin.

Joffe-Walt, Chana. 2015. "Three Miles." *This American Life* (March 13). www.thisamericanlife.org/radio-archives/episode/550/three-miles. Last accessed May 11, 2017.

Johnston, Peter. 2004. *Choice Words: How Our Language Affects Children's Learning*. Portland, ME: Stenhouse.

———. 2012. *Opening Minds: Using Language to Change Lives*. Portland, ME: Stenhouse.

Kahneman, Daniel. 2011. *Thinking, Fast and Slow*. New York: Farrar, Straus and Giroux.

Kant, Immanuel. 2012. *Idea for a Universal History with a Cosmopolitan Aim*, edited by James Schmidt and Amélie Oksenberg Rorty. Cambridge, England: Cambridge University Press.

Keats, John. 1899. *The Complete Poetical Works and Letters of John Keats*. Boston: Houghton, Mifflin and Company.

Kent, Richard. 2012. *Writing on the Bus*. New York: Peter Lang.

Kenyon, Jane. Nd. "Trouble with Math in a One-Room Country School." www.poetryfoundation.org/poetrymagazine/poems/detail/36164. Last accessed May 11, 2017.

Kinneavy, James. 1971. *A Theory of Discourse*. Englewood Cliffs, NJ: Prentice Hall.

Kohn, Alfie. 2001. "Five Reasons to Stop Saying 'Good Job!'" *Young Children* (September). www.alfiekohn.org/article/five-reasons-stop-saying-good-job/. Last accessed May 11, 2017.

Korn, Melissa. 2015. "Big Gap in College Graduation Rates for Rich and Poor, Study Finds." *Wall Street Journal* (February 3). www.wsj.com/articles/big-gap-in-college-graduation-rates-for-rich-and-poor-study-finds-1422997677. Last accessed May 11, 2017.

Kushner, Tony. 2011. *Lincoln*. www.imsdb.com/scripts/Lincoln.html. Last accessed May 11, 2017.

Leary, Mark R. 2004. *The Curse of the Self: Self Awareness, Egotism, and the Quality of Human Life*. Oxford, England: Oxford University Press.

Lindberg, Gary. 1986. "Case Study: A Scholar Writes and Reads." In *Read to Write: A Writing Process Reader*, edited by Donald Murray. New York: Holt.

Lockhart, Paul. 2009. *A Mathematician's Lament*. New York: Bellevue Literary Press.

Luria, Aleksandr R. 1968. *The Mind of a Mnemonist*. Cambridge, MA: Harvard University Press.

Machiavelli, Niccolo. 2001. *The Prince*. Translated by N. H. Thomson. New York: Bartelby.

Martínez, Tiffany. 2016. "Academia, Love Me Back." 2016. https://vivatiffany.wordpress.com/2016/10/27/academia-love-me-back/. Last accessed May 11, 2017.

Mead, George Herbert. 2015. *Mind, Self, and Society*. Chicago: University of Chicago Press.

Meyer, Dan. 2012. "These People with Their Dogs Wearing Bandanas." http://blog.mrmeyer.com/2012/these-people-with-their-dogs-wearing-bandanas/. Last accessed May 11, 2017.

———. 2010. "Math Class Needs a Makeover." TEDxNYED. www.ted.com/talks/dan_meyer_math_curriculum_makeover.html. Last accessed May 11, 2017.

Miller, Rowland S. 2007. "Is Embarrassment a Blessing or a Curse?" In *The Self-Conscious Emotions: Theory and Research*, edited by Jessica L. Tracy, Richard W. Robins, and June Price Tangney, 245–62. New York: Guilford.

Montaigne, Michel de. 1987. *The Complete Essays*. Translated and edited by M.A. Screech. New York: Penguin Books.

Morrison, Toni. 2007. *The Bluest Eye*. New York: Vintage.

Mukherjee, Siddhartha. 2011. *The Emperor of All Maladies: A Biography of Cancer.* New York: Scribner's.

Murray, Donald. 2009. "Teaching the Other Self: The Writer's First Reader." In *The Essential Don Murray: Lessons from America's Greatest Writing Teacher,* edited by Thomas Newkirk and Lisa C. Miller, 87–97. Portsmouth, NH: Heinemann.

Nelson-Le Gall, Sharon. 1985. "Help-Seeking Behavior in Learning." *Review of Research in Education* 12: 55–90.

Newkirk, Thomas. 1992. "Silences in Our Teaching Stories: What Do We Leave Out and Why?" In *Workshop 4: The Teacher as Researcher,* edited by Thomas Newkirk. Portsmouth, NH: Heinemann.

———. 2014. *Minds Made for Stories: How We Really Read and Write Informational and Persuasive Texts.* Portsmouth, NH: Heinemann.

———. 2015. "On the Virtue of Thinking Small: Reclaiming Teacher Research." In *The Teacher You Want to Be,* edited by Matt Glover and Ellin Oliver Keene. Portsmouth, NH: Heinemann.

Nietzsche, Friedrich. 1980. *On the Advantage and Disadvantage of History for Life.* Translated by Peter Preuss. Cambridge, MA: Hackett.

Nora, Julie. 2007. "Student Engagement in a 7th/8th Grade Social Studies, ESL Classroom." Dissertations and Master's Theses (Campus Access). Paper AAI3298375.

NPR Music. 2015. "For Iris Dement, Music Is the Calling That Forces Her into the Spotlight." www.npr.org/2015/10/21/450521621/for-iris-dement-music-is-the-calling-that-forces-her-into-the-spotlight. Last accessed May 11, 2017.

Nystrand, Martin, and Adam Gamoran. 1991. "Instructional Discourse, Student Engagement, and Literature Achievement." *Research in the Teaching of English* 25 (3): 261–90.

Ortmeier-Hooper, Christina. 2008. "English May Be My Second Language, but I'm Not 'ESL.'" *College Composition and Communication* 59 (3): 389–419.

———. 2013. *The ELL Writer: Moving Beyond Basics in the Secondary Classroom.* New York: Teachers College Press.

Orwell, George. 1998. "Reflections on Ghandi." *In A Collection of Essays,* 1349–57. New York: Everyman's Library.

Osnos, Evan. 2012. "Boss Rail." *The New Yorker* (October 22). www.newyorker.com/magazine/2012/10/22/boss-rail. Last accessed May 11, 2017.

Palmer, Amanda. 2013. "The Art of Asking." TED. www.youtube.com/watch?v=xMj_P_6H69g. Last accessed May 11, 2017.

PBS. 2002. "Misunderstood Minds: Writing Strategies." www.pbs.org/wgbh/misunderstoodminds/writingstrats.html. Last accessed May 11, 2017.

———. 2006. *Raising Cain*. DVD.

Pillemer, David. 1998. *Momentous Events, Vivid Memories*. Cambridge, MA: Harvard University Press.

———. 2001. "How Memories of School Experiences Can Enrich Educational Evaluations." In *New Directions for Evaluation: Evaluation Findings That Surprise*, edited by Richard J. Light. San Francisco: Jossey Bass.

Pillemer, David, M. L. Picariello, A. B. Law, and J. S. Reichman, 1996. "Memories of College: The Importance of Specific Educational Episodes." In *Remembering Our Past: Studies in Autobiographical Memory*, edited by David C. Rubin. New York: Cambridge University Press.

Pillemer, David, Kristina L. Steiner, Kie J. Kuwabara, D. K. Thomsen, and Connie Svob. 2015. "Vicarious Memories." *Consciousness and Cognition* 36: 233–45.

Pinker, Steven. 2014. *The Sense of Style: The Thinking Person's Guide to Writing in the 21st Century*. New York: Viking.

Plato. 1990. *The Phaedrus*. In *The Rhetorical Tradition: Readings from Classical Times to the Present*, edited by P. Bizzell and B. Hertzberg, 113–43. Boston: Bedford/St. Martins.

Pollan, Michael. 2008. *In Defense of Food: An Eater's Manifesto*. New York: Penguin.

Pomerance, Bernard. 1977. *The Elephant Man*. https://sites.google.com/site/mendomundo/home/bookshelf/the-elephant-man. Last accessed June 27, 2017.

Programme for International Student Assessment. 2014. "PISA 2012 Results in Focus: What 15-Year-Olds Know and What They Can Do with What They Know." www.oecd.org/pisa/keyfindings/pisa-2012-results-overview.pdf. Last accessed May 11, 2017.

Putnam, Robert. 2016. *Our Kids: The American Dream in Crisis*. New York: Simon and Schuster.

Ramirez-Esparza, Nairan, Adrian Garcia-Sierra, and Patricia K. Kuhl. 2014. "Look Who's Talking: Speech Style and Social Context in Language Input to Infants Are Linked to Concurrent and Future Speech Development." *Developmental Science* 16 (6): 880–91.

Roethke, Theodore. 1953. "The Waking." In *The Collected Poems of Theodore Roethke*. New York: Doubleday.

Roosevelt, Eleanor. 1960. *You Learn by Living*. New York: Harpers.

Rose, Mike. 1989. *Lives on the Boundary*. New York: The Free Press.

Sabini, John, Michael Siepmann, Julia Stein, and Marcia Meyerowitz. "Who Is Embarrassed by What?" *Cognition and Emotion* 14: 213–40.

Salinger, J. D. 1951. *The Catcher in the Rye*. New York: Little Brown.

Sapolsky, Robert M. 2004. *Why Zebras Don't Get Ulcers*, 3rd ed. New York: St. Martin's Griffin.

———. 2013. "The Appeal of Embarrassment." *The Wall Street Journal* (July 26). www.wsj.com/articles/SB10001424127887324564704578629823916370886. Last accessed May 11, 2107.

Schank, Roger. 1980. "Failure-Driven Memory." *Cognition and Brain Theory* 4: 41–60.

Seligman, Martin. 1998. *Learned Optimism: How to Change Your Life and Your Mind*. New York: Vintage.

Seneca. 2004. *Letters from a Stoic: Epistulae Morales ad Lucilium*. New York: Penguin.

Shakespeare, William. 1952a. *A Midsummer Night's Dream*. In *Shakespeare: The Complete Works*, edited by G. B. Harbison. New York: Harcourt, Brace, and World.

———. 1952b. *The Tragedy of King Lear*. In *Shakespeare: The Complete Works*, edited by G. B. Harbison. New York: Harcourt, Brace, and World.

Shaugnessy, Mina. 1977. *Errors and Expectations: A Guide for the Teacher of Basic Writing*. New York: Oxford University Press.

Stafford, William. 1990. "A Way of Writing." In *To Compose: Teaching Writing in High School and College*, Second Edition, edited by Thomas Newkirk. Portsmouth, NH: Heinemann.

Steele, Claude. 2011. *Whistling Vivaldi: How Stereotypes Affect Us and What We Can Do*. New York: Norton.

Sterne, Laurence. 1965. *The Life and Opinions of Tristram Shandy, Gentleman*. Boston: Houghton Mifflin.

Stigler, James. W., and James Hiebert. 2009. *The Teaching Gap: Best Ideas from the World's Teachers for Improving Education in the Classroom*. New York: Free Press.

Suskind, Ron. 2014. "Reaching My Autistic Son Through Disney." *New York Times Magazine* (March 7): MM, 20. www.nytimes.com/2014/03/09/magazine/reaching-my-autistic-son-through-disney.html?_r=0. Last accessed May 11, 2017.

Taylor, Shelly. 1989. *Positive Illusions: Creative Self-Deception and the Healthy Mind.* Boston: Basic Books.

Thaler, Richard H., and Cass R. Sunstein. 2009. *Nudge: Improving Decisions About Health, Wealth, and Happiness.* New York: Penguin.

Thoreau, Henry. 2000. *Walden and Civil Disobedience.* Boston: Houghton Mifflin.

Tomlinson, Brian. 2016. "Five Pieces of Advice to My Future Self (and Maybe You) About Speaking to Adult Language Learners." https://abcmerida.blogspot.mx/2016/08/advice-to-my-future-self-and-maybe-you.html. Last accessed May 11, 2017.

Tough, Paul. 2012. *How Children Succeed: Grit, Curiosity, and the Hidden Power of Character.* Boston: Houghton Mifflin, Harcourt.

———. 2016. "How Kids Learn Resilience." *The Atlantic* (June): 56–66.

Tyre, Peg. 2016. "The Math Revolution." *The Atlantic* (March). www.theatlantic.com/magazine/archive/2016/03/the-math-revolution/426855/. Last accessed May 11, 2017.

Umansky, Ilana M. 2016. "To Be or Not to Be EL: An Examination of the Impact of Classifying Students as English Learners." *Educational Evaluation and Policy Analysis.* http://metatoc.com/papers/87863-to-be-or-not-to-be-el-an-examination-of-the-impact-of-classifying-students-as-english-learners. Last accessed May 11, 2017.

Vygotsky, Lev. 1978. *Mind in Society.* Cambridge, MA: Harvard University Press.

———. 1986. *Thought and Language,* edited by Alex Kozulin. Cambridge, MA: Cambridge University Press.

Walmsley, Sean, and Richard Allington. 1995. "Redefining and Reforming Instructional Support Programs for At-Risk Students." In *No Quick Fix: Rethinking Literacy Programs in America's Public Schools,* edited by Richard Allington and Sean Walmsley, 19–44. New York: Teachers College Press.

Yutang, Li. 1935. *My Country and My People.* New York: Reynal and Hitchcock.

Zager, Tracy. 2017. *Becoming the Math Teacher You Wish You'd Had.* Portland, ME: Stenhouse.

INDEX

Q

R

S

Z